"Our character is what we do

when we think no one is looking."

-Quoted from P.S. I Love You

YOU'LL NEVER SPA
IN THIS TOWN AGAIN

ROBERT RANDOLPH

Published by Bluff Place Publishing

Los Angeles, CA

YOU'LL NEVER SPA

IN THIS TOWN AGAIN

Published in the United States by Bluff Place Publishing

ISBN-13: 978-0615451923

ISBN-10: 0615451926

CONTENTS

LIE DETECTOR TEST

In light of the James Frey / Oprah Winfrey scandal over Frey's so-called memoir, *A Million Little Pieces*, so many of us have become skeptical and wary of the endless, and often dubious, memoirs and tell-alls that are flooding the market these days. Simply put, today's readers have the right to know what is true and what is fabricated. I wanted my book to stand out and have real validity with my readers. With this in mind, I hired an independent polygraph examiner to attest to the accuracy and truthfulness of my book—a book that I wrote from my own personal experiences and events that I witnessed firsthand! I want to make it perfectly clear to everyone that *You'll Never Spa in This Town Again* is a *true* autobiographical, nonfiction memoir from start to finish, and I challenge anyone to prove otherwise!

Sincerely,
Author Robert Randolph

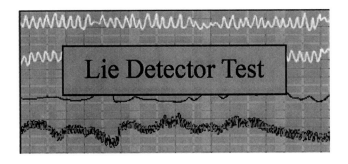

1. Were you a member of the spas you wrote about in your book?   Yes

2. Were you completely honest about the stars you wrote about?   Yes

3. Were you brutally attacked at City Spa by Warren Smith, a fellow spa member?   Yes

4. Did you exaggerate or make up any parts of your book *You'll Never Spa in This Town Again*?   No

5. Did you see John Travolta having gay sex at Century Spa while his son, Jett, waited for him in the car?   Yes

6. Did Warren Smith attack you a second time at City Spa?   Yes

7. Before these events happened to you, were you planning on writing a book about the spas?   No

8. Did you personally meet every star that you wrote about in your book? — Yes

9. Have you repeatedly witnessed John Travolta in lewd sexual acts at the spas? — Yes

10. Were you shown a videotape that showed John Travolta engaged in sex with a man? — Yes

11. Did John Travolta proposition you for sex on more than one occasion? — Yes

12. Did you see George Michael engaging in anal intercourse with another man? — Yes

14. Have you received multiple death threats regarding the release of your book? — Yes

15. John Travolta's attorney, Marty Singer, claims that you were institutionalized. Were you? — No

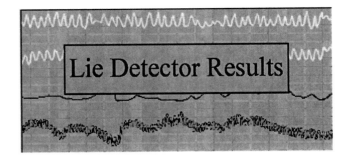

Conclusion:

"After carefully reviewing the polygraph charts of the subject (Robert Randolph), it is the opinion of this examiner, that there was no indication of deception during the polygraph examination."

-From the report of the polygraph examiner I worked with on September 22, 2011

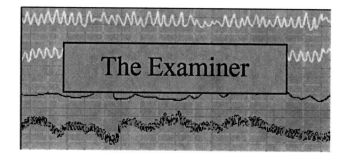

The Examiner

When the time came for me to get my polygraph test done for the book, I was very selective of whom I wanted to do the exam. I knew I wanted someone with an extensive background in the field, and that is exactly who I found. He is one of the top polygraph examiners in the world.

He was once a U.S. Secret Service special agent. He also worked the Protective Service Detail for the white house and remained there long enough to have four different presidents as his superior. He has over sixteen thousand polygraph examinations under his belt and has testified in both state and federal courts. He is trusted by state and federal public defenders' offices to perform polygraph tests and he is called on often to review the polygraph examinations conducted by law enforcement agencies to see if there were carried out properly. This is a mere partial list of the accomplishments he has achieved during his long and highly revered career to say the least.

I had originally planned to name the examiner in my book, and he was happy to be included, but after some thought, I decided against it.

Packin' or Lackin'

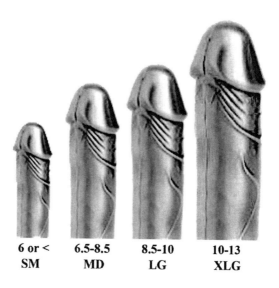

6 or <	6.5-8.5	8.5-10	10-13
SM	MD	LG	XLG

My definition of Packin' or Lackin' is my personal opinion regarding the size of the male penis. Keep in mind that size, much like beauty, is in the eye of the beholder. Well, since I have had plenty of opportunities to behold these celebrity's penises while they were exposed to me, I have come up with this little rating system.

DEDICATION

Dedicated to Nate.

The guard at the gate,

And the keeper of the secrets

For so many years at City Spa.

To me, you will always be my hero

And the angel who saved my life.

I would not be here today if it were not for you.

I owe you my life.

You always said that people who spoke

Of things that went on at City Spa

Have ended up at the bottom of a river.

You also used to say,

What happens at City Spa, stays at City Spa.

Forgive me, Nate,

Not this time.

AUTHOR'S NOTES

I was born and raised in Inglewood, California. I have lived in Los Angeles all my life. My grandfather, Joseph Robinson, was a key grip for 20th Century Fox Studios for over four decades. His uncle Charlie ran the studio. My grandfather's life revolved around the studio, making movies, and drinking with all his buddies—Barbara Stanwyck, Mae West, Bette Davis, Joan Crawford, Marilyn Monroe, Betty Grable, and John Wayne, to name a few. He especially adored Humphrey Bogart and Spencer Tracy. If you were a movie star and making movies at Fox Studios, you were more than likely my grandfather's drinking buddy. Grandpa Joe, as he was called, was friends with all of them. When filming was done for the day, everyone, from the movie stars in front of the camera, as well as all the people behind the scenes, would get drunk and play cards together on set. There was no discriminating from the stars and the regulars. They all drank together. They were like a big family.

As a kid, I had no concept of movie stars. My grandmother, Dorothy Robinson, would pick up my grandfather at the studio after work most of the days. Most days I would go with her. He would never be in front of the studio as he was supposed to be. We would always have to go onto the studio lot and try to find Grandpa. I loved it—my grandmother did not. We would wander from one movie set to another. It was so fascinating to me when we would eventually find Grandpa. He would be drunk, playing cards with Stanwyck and Bogart, or whomever he had been working with on that particular day.

Growing up in that circle, I learned there was a secret code between the regulars and the movie stars, in which as long as you did not speak of the celebrity and kept their life private, you would remain close. It was a strict code. When someone would break that code, you were out. And out for good! Grandma and I would eventually locate Grandpa. She would start drinking with them and join the party, and the party usually would last until the wee hours of the morning. I spent many a night as a child sleeping on the set of what would later become a famous movie. Eventually, my grandparents would wake me up, and we would go home. My grandparents were always the last to leave. Therefore, to grow up and be around the famous movie stars in L.A., or at my spa, was just normal to me.

Now let me tell you what is not the norm. That is, to do it and then write a book about it. To tell all you have seen, all you have been told, and the dirty secrets these movie stars have exposed to you. I am breaking the secret code. Here, I am writing about the movie stars who have shared deep secrets with me. I know I will no longer be in the circle, but I feel confident that after you read my story, you will understand my reasoning and motivation behind my book *You'll Never Spa in This Town Again.*

INTRODUCTION

The year was 1975, and ABC had all the popular hits: *Happy Days*, *Mork & Mindy*, *The Love Boat*, *Fantasy Island*, and *Welcome Back, Kotter*. Every chance I got, I was in front of our television, watching all the shows, trying to escape my suburban boredom. I would never miss my favorite show, *Welcome Back, Kotter*, because of John Travolta. He was the breakaway actor who made that show a hit, not to mention he had a number one hit record, and it seemed like he was on the cover of every single magazine. The whole world was in love with John Travolta, and I was no exception. He was overexposed, but I had no complaints. I was so excited when I learned he had an upcoming movie coming out called *Saturday Night Fever*. This movie was supposed to be phenomenal. There was also talk that John's dancing in the movie was going to change dancing forever and that this movie was going to make John Travolta the biggest movie star in the world.

Travolta was all around me. I watched him on television every chance I got, and I listened to his music album until the needle wore out. If that wasn't enough, I bought every single magazine or book his face was on. I was completely under his movie star spell. I had one problem, though, and to me, at thirteen years of age it was huge. *Saturday Night Fever* was going to be rated R. I hated that rating because it was the only thing standing between John Travolta and me. How was I going to get someone to get me in? My parents were definitely out of the question. What adult would take me to a movie that was filled with sex and bad words...everything I wasn't even supposed to think about at that age. Yeah, right!

I had one possibility, and that was my grandparents. *It can't get better than this,* I thought. My grandparents were perfect. They were alcoholics. Now, on the weekends, they would really get drunk. If I spent the weekend over at their home, they would not even notice what movie they were going to or watching. I concocted this whole scheme where I told them *Saturday Night Fever* was like the musical *The Sound of Music,* which was my grandmother's all-time favorite movie. I added that I heard it was going to be a real solid family movie. I was lying through my teeth, but I did not care because I would have said anything to get there. I just had to be there opening weekend. Therefore, I prepped Grandma that week because I wanted her ready for the weekend. It was getting close, and all I could think about was John Travolta and *Saturday Night Fever.* I was going to be there.

The weekend came, and Grandma was so sure this movie was going to be a hit, like *The Sound of Music*, that she planned a special surprise for me. She invited my cousins, knowing I always had fun with them. The problem for me now was that my grandparents were always sober and on their best behavior around them. You see, my cousins Mike and Chris were direct descendants of Saint Barbara, my grandmother's middle daughter, who could do no wrong. Every time my grandmother would say Barbara's name, she would make the sign of the cross. Therefore, I knew things were going to get messy. In addition, my grandparents would know that I had lied to them because they were going to be sober all day! Off we went to the movie theater. I knew at this point I would have hell to pay, but I could not have cared less. I would not have changed a thing except, of course, I wished they were drunk.

My grandmother and grandfather sat directly behind me, and the movie started. *Wow*, there was a lot of cussing. "Fuck this and fuck that," and when they weren't saying it, they were doing it. My grandma was mortified at what she was seeing and hearing on the big screen. She was equally as livid because she was in this theater expecting to see what she believed was this wonderful movie, she had invited my cousins and everything, just to find out she had been tricked, and to top it off, she was missing out on a weekend of drinking. Worst of all, it was because of me that my saintly cousins were being exposed to such dirty filth.

My grandma was yanking at my hair every time she heard or saw something vulgar. "Shame on you, Robby!" she would scream as she pulled my hair. I could hear her repeatedly saying, "Oh, this is filthy!"

This yanking and nagging went on for about an hour. Either I fainted or my grandma pulled me out of the theater by my hair. I don't remember. However, what I do remember is, as I was leaving the movie theater that day, there was the *Saturday Night Fever* life-sized cutout of John Travolta wearing that famous white suit and striking that famous pose. As I looked him in the eyes on that cutout, I had this feeling that someday I would know him.

It would be years until I saw the rest of *Saturday Night Fever*. I rented it when it came out on VHS, and I watched it without the painful yanking of my hair by my grandmother. I was sitting on my sofa, in peace, watching John Travolta dance his way into my heart. He did something to me. I wanted to be like him and act like him. I wanted to know how to dance like him, too, after watching John Travolta do the famous dance scenes in the movie. He left me mesmerized. I would spend hours and hours dancing in front of the mirror, practicing all the moves to the dances he did in *Saturday Night Fever*. I really wore out the soundtrack. On the weekend, I would go out dancing with my friends at Disneyland. We all thought we were as cool as John Travolta was. It would be a long time until we realized we were not.

Chapter 1

TRAVOLTA ENCOUNTER
December 4, 1993

It was Friday, December 4, 1993. My thirtieth birthday was the next day.

I had rented the Presidential Suite at the Beverly Hills Hilton Hotel, "Merv Griffin's Place," for the entire weekend. Yes! What a weekend it was going to be.

I had invited approximately fifty friends to celebrate turning thirty years old. I checked into the hotel on Friday, and immediately turned the Presidential Suite into my own world.

I brought some personal effects from home, such as pictures, music, et cetera. As soon as I filled the suite with tons of flowers and had everything just the way I wanted it, my home away from home, I headed out to Neiman Marcus, my favorite department store in the world. After spending a couple of hours shopping, I went to the valet to pick up my car.

While waiting for my car, I turned around and ran smack-dab into John Travolta. He was coming from around the corner, and we literally smacked into each other. Our eyes met and locked.

"Well, hello there!" he said.

I just freaked.

He put his hand out to introduce himself to me, "I'm John Travolta," as if I didn't know. I introduced myself, and he just stood there staring at me.

I couldn't believe it. John Travolta was flirting with me. For the first time, I knew he was gay by his body language with me. I was in shock! All the rumors were true, and I had just witnessed it for myself.

He was so sweet and flirty with me. It was the perfect surprise gift for my thirtieth birthday. Meeting my favorite movie star, John Travolta, and to find out, for sure, he was gay.

I told myself one day I was going to know that man, and we were going to be close. As quick as it began, it was over. He said he had to get a few Christmas gifts inside the store, winked at me, and left. I stood there watching him leave and could not help but think how gorgeous he was in person.

My whole body was excited. Just before he was out of view, I noticed he looked back at me and waved again. I waved back, and he was gone. I wondered if I should go into Neiman's after him, but just then, the valet pulled up in my car, so I decided to leave and let Travolta shop in peace.

Later on, I would regret not taking the chance that he had given me. Instead of going in and seeing what was up, I froze. It all happened so unexpectedly that I didn't have a chance to think. I shared the story with my party guests the next night.

"I blew it; I should have followed Travolta's lead and at least found out if there was more he wanted from me. However, as I said, I froze."

Even as I told the story, something inside me kept saying, *You'll have many more chances with John Travolta*, so I left it at that.

The weekend was a blast, and Mr. Travolta was the icing on the cake for my thirtieth birthday. Little did I know my wait to run into John Travolta would not be too long at all.

Chapter 2

FOLLOWING A RUMOR

It was 1995, and I was living a great life. I had a beautiful oceanfront home in the South Bay. I was in my early thirties, and I felt like I had it all, except for a lover. Other than that, I was happy.

L.A. has always been a hot spot, but Long Beach was closer, so that was where I hung out with my friends. On occasion, we would go to the clubs in L.A., and every time we did, we always ran into guys who were talking about John Travolta. You know, how he was gay and if you wanted to meet him, it was really easy to do, et cetera, et cetera.

On one of my trips to L.A., this guy named Farrell shared his story. "I hooked up with John numerous times at local spas. John is a very lonely man. He needs a good boyfriend so he can stop all his cruising."

"I've always had a crush on John Travolta, and I would love to meet him," I quickly responded.

"You remind me of Travolta a lot."

"I've heard that plenty of times. Do you think John would like me?"

"If you have a dick, John Travolta will like you."

"Is he really that much of a whore?"

"Yes, but it's only because he's so lonely. I know because he told me."

"Then why aren't you with John?"

"My dick is not big enough to keep John's attention for more than a few minutes," he said truthfully.

No man goes around selling himself short in the dick department, so I had a strong feeling he had to be telling the truth. I guess this is when I started fantasizing about meeting John Travolta and how I would fall in love with him, and he with me.

As I said, by now I had been hearing these rumors for years about John being gay. No matter where I went, I would run into people who would tell me their story about meeting John Travolta at a spa and then having sex with him, so they said.

I still only halfway believed all these guys, but then I would read something in a tabloid, and it would confirm for me they were telling the truth. The stories were always about hookups in steam rooms, with everyone saying the same thing. There just had to be some truth to it, and I wanted to find out for myself firsthand.

I told myself I'd meet him one day and pretty much left it at that, until one time Farrell called me on the phone and told me John Travolta's new favorite place to go and steam for hookups was this spa called City Spa, and that if I still wanted to meet my crush, John Travolta, I should go there and start hanging out. I thanked him for the insider information and said that I would call him after I went there. Even though I definitely had a crush on John Travolta and wanted to meet him, I still did not get around to going to City Spa for a while.

The biggest reason was I was busy living in the real world, and no matter how fun and exciting meeting John Travolta sounded, I truly believed the likelihood and probability of it happening was bullshit. I could not believe in a million years John Travolta, this huge movie star, was a spa pervert available to anyone in the spa for sex. It was too far-fetched, but it was a fun fantasy. So, in a way, the fantasy was good enough at the time, and that is how I left it...as a fantasy.

I would think about going to City Spa all the time. Surprisingly, I would not go for months. When I did finally get ready to go, I gave Farrell a call.

"I can't believe that you still haven't gone yet. I thought you were serious about meeting Travolta?"

"I am. I've just been busy."

"Since we last talked, I sucked John's dick three times at City Spa. He's there almost every day, for hours, getting massages and then cruising the steam rooms for hookups afterwards."

"I'm heading there today," I assured him.

"Be prepared to have your mind blown, and possibly your dick, too."

I was ready to meet him, but I kept thinking...*Could he really be such a cruising cock whore? Is he really as filthy as everyone is saying?*

If he was, I wondered if I would even like him after meeting him. Promiscuous is one thing; sex addict is another. While calling City Spa and getting information about the services they offered, I was thinking and joking to myself, *Is John Travolta one of the services you offer at your spa?* But, of course, I did not mention his name. I booked a massage and got directions to the spa. Within minutes of getting off the phone, I was out the door and headed to the twilight zone.

Chapter 3

CITY SPA

It's only right that I start my book with Milena. If it weren't for Milena's influence on me, her keen sense of intuition, and, ultimately, her game plan to make me into John Travolta's boyfriend...this book would be a lot shorter and a lot less entertaining.

I met Milena the very first day I went to City Spa. I had heard several rumors that John Travolta was a regular there and on any given day, for the price of admission, you could go in and take a steam bath, naked, and John Travolta might just be there.

Well, he was not there the first day, but Milena was.

I entered the spa, paid the admission, and booked a one-hour massage. What luck! By luck, I mean this: Milena, who apparently knew everything there was to know about Travolta, was to be my masseuse. My number one reason for going to City Spa was to meet John Travolta, first as a fan, and then I wanted to see if there was any truth to the constant rumors that he was having sex at spas. So by luck, I meant really lucky!

The very first thing Milena said to me when I met her upstairs for my massage was, "John Travolta is going to love you, baby!"

I could not believe my ears. I hadn't said one word to her, especially not a word about Travolta, and here she was, telling me this.

She immediately followed it up with, "Of course, you need a complete makeover from head to toe, and you need to lose at least seventy-five pounds."

I just listened, then I asked a million questions, and she had answers for every one of them. She truly knew John Travolta, and I could not help but feel extremely lucky to have met her.

Milena is a big-boned Russian woman, with huge, strong hands that know how to truly massage. Her hair is blonde, long, and from the moment you meet her, you like her. She has a real strong personality, and she talks with a strong Russian accent.

It did not take me long to realize that I had just met my new best friend, and that is exactly what we became, BFFs. But, as with most things, the "forever" part didn't last, but nonetheless, I have nothing but wonderful, fun-filled memories of Milena and her scheme to make me John Travolta's boyfriend.

She was right; I did need to lose seventy-five pounds. I had injured my back two years prior, and before I knew it, I had packed on seventy-five pounds. She also wanted me to get my teeth capped. She had a game plan, and within one week of meeting Milena, I was putting it into action. Oh yes, and her biggest demand was that John Travolta was not to lay eyes on me until I was completely transformed. She told me she would put together the list of things I needed to get done. The list went something like this: lose seventy-five pounds, get a trainer and replace the fat with muscles, completely make over my teeth, including caps, grow my hair out, stop smoking, and start tanning. This list of Milena's went on and on.

After taking it all in and looking at all the procedures and physical changes that she came up with…I could see it would be quite a while until I met Mr. Travolta. However, Milena assured me it would be worth the wait, and when he finally saw me, he would take one look at me, fall in love, and stop being so promiscuous at the spa. She went on to say she was worried Travolta was going to get caught having sex at the spa, and all he really needed was a good-looking guy with a good heart as his boyfriend. She was sure if he had a good man, he would stop his cruising ways. Milena also said everyone at the spa felt Travolta was a very lonely man and I would be just what he needed. I could not believe my ears. Everything she was saying was so exciting and unexpected. I had come to the spa following a rumor about Travolta, and now, on my first visit, this masseuse was blowing my mind with her game plan to set me up with him. She also assured me he was not going anywhere and that she would personally mold me into his perfect man.

Another thing Milena said to me that first day when I disrobed was, "Oh, baby, John Travolta is going to love your dick." That was the only part of my anatomy she liked just the way it was.

I asked her, "How would you know what kind of dick John likes?"

Her reply? "Trust me; I know he likes them real big, just like yours." She went on to tell me about this doctor client of hers, Dr. Bryan. "Dr. Bryan's dick looks just like yours, and Travolta has been after that dick for years."

She stated how Dr. Bryan was completely straight and repulsed by all of Travolta's passes at him. Apparently, Travolta had offered him a lot of money if he would become his "down-low" boyfriend. Dr. Bryan's answer was a flat-out *no*. She said it had gotten to the point that whenever Dr. Bryan would see Travolta in the spa, the doctor would go in the opposite direction to avoid him.

I could not believe what a wealth of knowledge she was. By the time she had finished my massage, she had mapped out everything. Since Milena had worked at City Spa for years, she knew everything going on in that place. Milena didn't know it, but I had already made plans to buy a membership, and even though I did not live close to the spa, I was excited to be in my shoes...which I would be exchanging for running shoes. I had no idea it would end up taking years before I would finally reach all my goals.

She said, "Whenever Travolta comes in, I'll call you, and you can come in and spy on him, of course, without being seen."

Therefore, that is what I did, hundreds of times, during the makeover period. She would call and say, "Travolta's in the house!"

That's what all the employees would say whenever John Travolta was on the premises. Boy, would City Spa come to life! Everyone, including fellow spa members, would be on alert because Travolta was "in the house."

It was a difficult task watching him from afar and not letting him see me. I wanted, so many times, just to go up to him and say hi, as I witnessed so many do over the course of several years, but I did not stray from Milena's game plan. There would be no meeting John Travolta until I was completely revamped, so I stayed in the shadows. I worked out hard every day, because, in my mind, at the end of this program, I would be introduced to the world's biggest movie star, whom I just so happened to adore. Therefore, it was all worth it to me. All the miles I ran, all the dental surgeries to get my teeth fixed, all the weights I lifted, and all the food and drink I turned down. Yes, all worth it. It seemed like a very small price to pay for such a grand opportunity.

Milena said, no matter how hard she tried over the years, Travolta would not let her give him a massage. All the masseuses and masseurs knew that Travolta would not allow a woman to touch him. She made me promise when I finally landed Travolta that I would make him experience her massage. I agreed and said, "Of course."

Chapter 4

SEVENTY-FIVE POUNDS

Everything Milena said to me during my first massage was true. Who was I kidding? This was John Travolta, the world's biggest movie star. What would he want with an obese guy, when he could have anyone he wanted? It was a real eye-opener for me to see how much weight I had put on. *Wow!* Almost exactly one hundred pounds overweight! I knew this effort to lose the weight would take a lot longer than Milena was thinking.

Even though in the past I had been able to drop the pounds in no time when I put my mind to it, this time I was staring at a scale that indicated I needed to lose seventy-five pounds. When I did the math, I knew it would take me at least a year. On top of the weight loss, she wanted me to build muscles onto my frame. That just meant it was going to take even more time. Depressing to say the least, but on the flip side, getting in shape to meet John Travolta was very exciting and certainly worth the effort.

I felt like it was a win-win situation. If he didn't like me "that way" when he met me, I'd at least be a brand-new man in every way, from head to toe and *A* to *Z*, so how could I lose? More than anything, it was all so surreal, exciting, and straight out of some crazy movie starring John Travolta and me.

I was impatient and wished I could meet John then, but I knew the truth…He would not have given me the time of day, so I had to get real with myself. Once I did that, I set my game plan.

Depressed? What depression? I was on my way to an amazing adventure.

Now just the mere thought of a visit to the dentist made me shake with extreme fear. I didn't know how I was going to toughen my way through this whole mouth makeover. The thought of capping all my teeth scared me to death. Not that I didn't need to, I was just deathly afraid of the dentist. But I knew it had to be done. Therefore, through the grace of God, I found the most amazing dentist in the world, Dr. Aris Corkos. He made me feel right at ease, and he knew how to handle a tough-guy baby like me. If you have ever had a bad experience with a dentist that left you paralyzed with fear, then you will understand where I was coming from. I could have never faced my dental fears without Dr. Corkos. The whole dental transformation would end up taking about fourteen months to complete. It was tough because, just my luck, I had a lot of extra work that needed to be done.

The outcome was amazing, and in the end, after nearly a year and a half, my mouth was beautiful.

Under the guidance of Milena, I enlisted the help of one of the top trainers at the Easton Gym in West Hollywood. This gym has been around a long time, and all the stars have gone there. When I first started working out there, it was so much fun because I was on the same schedule of going to the gym as Patrick Dempsey, as he was just starting his unbelievable comeback. He was a really nice guy in person, very short in stature, though. I was actually shocked at how short he was.

I would go to Easton's every day to do cardio, and every other day I had workouts with my trainer, Joe. After losing so much weight, I was a little flabby. I definitely had to do something about it, so I relentlessly stuck with my program. Never swaying or cheating, no sick days for me back then. I was seeing results fast. With every day, I became stronger and more confident in myself for all I had accomplished. Things were looking up to say the least.

Everyone I ran across was telling me how great I looked. In addition, at City Spa, all the masseuses, and even the members, were asking, "How did you lose so much weight?" and "What can I do to look as good as you do?" It was very touching the way people went out of their way to acknowledge all my efforts.

"The Atkins diet, plus a lot of working out," I would tell them.

People were saying that I had inspired them to get in shape. My ego was growing on a daily basis, and for the first time in my life, I was truly at peace with my appearance. And why not? After all I did to change it!

Chapter 5

KAMBIZ

The hardest part about my scheme to meet Travolta was putting up with the owner of City Spa, Kambiz. If I had not been so set on what I was doing, I would have never returned to the spa after the first time I saw Kambiz degrade someone. I tried with all I had to stomach the horrible man.

Whenever Travolta would come in, Kambiz would announce to all the staff, "Travolta is in the house," and the word spread fast. There was electricity in the air when Travolta was there; you could definitely feel it.

Those were my, as well as everyone else's, favorite times at City Spa, when you would hear "Travolta is in the house." It was like Christmas Day. Everyone was on their best behavior and wanted to be near him.

Kambiz typically escorted Travolta through the spa so they could be seen together. Kambiz would introduce important members to Travolta to impress them. One time, Kambiz joined John in a steam in the Russian Room. I was in the Russian Room, relaxing, and I could not believe my eyes when I looked up and saw that Kambiz and Travolta were coming in. I threw my extra towel over my head and prayed they would sit at the other end from me. They did! I hunched down and watched while making sure Travolta did not see me. My heart was pounding, and I was already hot from the steam. I would not be able to last too long before I would have to step out for air and cool down. However, that meant walking right in front of Travolta! It was quite a dilemma at the time, I felt like I was going to pass out from heat exposure! While they sat there together, Kambiz treated John like a star, giving him the real movie star treatment. As members would come into the Russian Room, Kambiz would introduce Travolta to the ones he felt deserved to meet him. Everyone acted impressed and star struck upon meeting the *Saturday Night Fever* star.

On this particular night, there were mostly Russian members in the steam room. When John got up to exit, everyone sat up and said good-bye, including Kambiz. As soon as John was gone, Kambiz started making fun of him. He bent over in front of us all, parted his ass cheeks, and said, "Hi, I'm John Travolta. Do you want to fuck me in my ass?"

All the Russians started laughing. The same bunch who had just met John and acted so impressed with him were now mocking him, like Kambiz, by parting their cheeks open and saying the same things.

I could not believe my eyes, and I could not believe how two-faced Kambiz was. I wanted so badly to go up to

John and tell him that these people were not his friends, but I had not met him yet, and it went against Milena's game plan. I ultimately knew if I did such a thing, my days at City Spa would be over, so I kept my mouth shut.

The sadness I felt for Travolta that night would stay with me for a long time. I kept thinking how sad his life truly was. There he was, a man who appeared to have it all, and the truth was, he did not. He lurked around steam rooms and saunas, looking for sex like a complete sex addict. Everyone who worked at the spas knew what Travolta was up to. He was not fooling anyone. And he hadn't for a long time.

To my face, Kambiz was nice. He knew I dumped a ton of money at his spa, and he treated me that way, but all the employees would tell me a different story of how Kambiz really talked about me. It was no surprise to me at all. After the way I had seen him treat others, I expected no different.

You never knew what kind of mood Kambiz would be in. For the most part, he was always in a foul mood, and he seemed to take a great joy in sharing it with everyone. Kambiz was always either firing someone or accusing another of stealing. He never stopped his rage, except, of course, for the few minutes when a new member might be there, or if someone was looking over the spa to join it. He would be all cheery and phony for the moment, but it never lasted.

As I said, if I was not so set on my game plan, I never would have joined City Spa back in 1995 with such a rottento-the-core owner, but I was, and I did. In early 2003, after years and years of purchasing one-year memberships, my membership was up for renewal again, and this time, I decided to purchase three one-year memberships from City Spa instead: one for myself and one each for two of my closest friends, Boris and Ilya.

When I purchased the memberships from Nate (the person I have dedicated this book to), I specifically told him not to deposit the check for one week, as I told him the funds would not be in my account until then. He said he understood and said he would hold the check personally until then so it would not be accidentally deposited. I thanked him and went on my way.

Next thing I know, I'm hearing that my check to City Spa has bounced and Kambiz was telling everyone at the spa, employees and members, that I had written him a bad check. All of a sudden, members I knew were asking me if I needed a loan to cover my membership. I could not believe what I was hearing, so I immediately went to talk to Nate and asked him what was up. Nate said that when he told Kambiz that I had purchased the memberships, Kambiz asked him where the money was. Nate said he told him about our arrangement.

"Bullshit, that motherfucker is rich! He has the money in his account, and you had better deposit it immediately," Kambiz retorted.

Nate said he pleaded with him, but to no avail.

Kambiz said, "You deposit it now, or you're fired!"

Therefore, Nate did, and it bounced. Kambiz went on to tell everyone that I was a thief and that I had tried to rob him, but Nate stuck up for me and told many of the members and staff that it was not true. Even so, from then on, a lot of them looked at me as a shady bad check writer. Nate went out of his way to repeatedly apologize to me, and I knew in my heart he was sincere.

He said, "Rob, we hold checks all the time like I was doing for you. Kambiz just wanted to have something he could use against you to make you look bad."

I never held Nate responsible, and when the check was put through the second time, of course it cleared. By this time, I had been a member of City Spa for years. It had truly become my second home. I worked out there, steamed there, ate there, made many friends there, et cetera, et cetera. At this point, in 2003, I had put away my silly plans of Travolta and me years ago. These three one-year memberships would be the last time I renewed my membership at City Spa. Besides, if I had not gone forward and purchased the memberships, Kambiz would have forever tainted my name, and everything he accused me of would have appeared to be true and evident with me no longer going to the spa. Therefore, I decided right then and there to forget about the asshole owner, Kambiz, and not let him ruin my reputation. Somehow or another, he would get what was coming to him, and I did not have to worry about it, because everyone hated him.

Anyway, I moved on, but that episode would follow me forever. In fact, the night Warren Smith was trying to murder me, he kept saying to me as he was beating my brains out, "Who do you think you are, writing the spa a bad check, you motherfucker?"

First, I couldn't believe that Warren Smith, a member at City Spa, was trying to kill me, and second, I couldn't believe what he was saying to me. I thought, *Oh my God! Is he going to kill me over that story Kambiz told everyone that was, in fact, a lie? Am I going to die here on Pico Boulevard because of Kambiz?*

It was pure insanity to be at the receiving end of all of Warren's cocaine-fueled rage that night, but that is where I found myself. For whatever reason, Warren chose those words to say as he beat my brains out, literally.

As I could distinctly hear the metal inside that sock banging into my skull, I could also hear Warren screaming, "Who do you think you are, Rob, fucking around with John Travolta's business? You ugly faggot, you're not Travolta's type, and he doesn't want you!"

Again my mind was racing. Why was he bringing up John Travolta to me while he was beating me? In addition, how would he know what John thought of me unless John had told him? It was horrible, and Kambiz was behind it all. Or so I was told.

I was told that after Nate carried me into the lobby, and I was lying there dying, Kambiz's only concern was to clean up the blood from the attack before the police and ambulance arrived. He is a coldhearted man, and if it were up to him, he would have left me on Pico Boulevard to die while he locked his spa door.

Luckily, for me, God had other plans for me that night, and I am here to tell you I am glad he did, because if Nate had not burst through the doors to save me, Warren would have succeeded in killing me, and no one would have ever known it was him. I have thought a million times of how it could have played out differently to Warren's favor and not mine.

As if going through an attack that left me beaten unconscious wasn't bad enough, Kambiz's actions would bring further life-threatening harm my way. The police could not locate Warren Smith after the incident, and Kambiz knew Warren was wanted by the authorities. The detectives working the case had been to City Spa several times to talk to Kambiz and others about Warren Smith, so everyone knew what was going on. Yet when I would return to the spa a few months later to face my fears, instead of protecting me, Kambiz once again subjected me to Warren's rage.

When I arrived to the spa on December 8, 2003, Kambiz was working the front desk. He did not say one thing to me. No acknowledgement at all. Not "I'm so sorry for what you went through." Nothing! To add insult to injury, Kambiz allowed Warren back into the spa without notifying either the police or me. Even more heinous was the fact that, on that fateful day when I entered the spa, Kambiz knew that Warren was there and made no mention whatsoever of his presence. He is a very mean and vindictive man. He let me go in knowing full well Warren was in the spa.

I entered the spa, disrobed, grabbed a towel, and left my locker for the steam room. My stomach was in knots being in the spa, but I wanted to push through the fear instilled in me from the last time I had been there. As I entered the steam room, it was full of steam, and I could not see anything. Then, suddenly, I could see, and I could not believe what I saw before me. It was Warren Smith, and again, he was coming straight for me.

I wanted to believe what I was seeing was an illusion, a mind trick of some sort. However, I knew better than to waste time pondering and ran with everything I had. I ran as fast as I could. I did not know what it was that he was holding, but whatever it was, he was coming straight for me with it in his hand. I ran, screaming and begging for help, and somehow, I was able to escape from Warren this time.

I made my way out the front door, onto Pico Boulevard, naked. Warren was still right behind me. I could not believe it! No one was helping me, and I could not believe this was happening again at my beloved City Spa, but it was, and this time it was broad daylight. As I rounded the corner to the City Spa parking lot, I screamed for Ray, the parking lot attendant, to call the police because Warren was trying to kill me again. When I reached the parking lot and the safety of my parked car, Warren could see he was not going to get me this time, and he took off in another direction.

As I sat there naked and in full shock, and shaking beyond belief, Ray tried to console me. He kept saying, "How could Kambiz let Warren back into the spa when he knows the police are after him for the first time he attacked you and nearly killed you?"

I had no answer, absolutely no answer. When the police arrived and went into City Spa to talk to Kambiz, he had already left the spa through a back exit. He was nowhere to be found. What could Kambiz have against me so strongly that he would knowingly and intentionally put my life at risk again?

I didn't know the answer then, and I still don't, but I knew nothing would ever be the same with me and City Spa again. It was finally over.

I came to the realization that these people were not my friends. There was no City Spa family. It was all an illusion, from John Travolta and everything in between, that I encountered at City Spa. The only thing that was real was the brain trauma I suffered from the attack and all the post-trauma suffering that came with it.

I knew that whatever time I spent at City Spa from there on out , I'd be on a new mission, and that would be to bring to light the truth of the illegal drug dealing and usage at City Spa and all the sexual hookups that were going down—especially among all the celebrities living double lives who Kambiz allowed to use his spa for their own sexual playground.

Somehow, someway, I knew I would pay Kambiz back for all he had done to all his employees and me over the years. The best part was all I had to do was tell the truth about everything I had witnessed and been through with City Spa. After all, I always thought if anybody ever wrote a book about that place, no one would believe it. Or would they?

A close source recently told me Kambiz had gotten wind about my book and said, "That motherfucker Rob is writing a book about City Spa? If he goes through with it, everyone from Travolta to the gangsters that go there will have it in for him." Kambiz went on to elaborate that one of them would kill me or have me killed.

Kambiz went on to tell my source that the last guy who was writing a book about City Spa was found at the bottom of a river, with anchors tied to his legs, and the same would come of me.

We all know the more money you have, the more power you have. I know Kambiz and Travolta have the power to kill me. In addition, as for Kambiz, his threats against my life are documented. The attacks that took place at City Spa are as well. So for now, I bask in the thought that I never have to see that horrible man's face again…Kambiz.

Chapter 6

FUN IN THE SUN

If I were to take a guess at what was crazier at City Spa, with my choices being the steam rooms or the rooftop sundeck, it would be hard to do. They are neck and neck in terms of bad-boy behavior. On any given day, you could escape the city and its bustle below for a rooftop sexual interlude.

Over the years, I have witnessed a lot of guys in the act of sexual misconduct on that sundeck. Seems the last thing anyone was looking for was the sun. It always amazed me how these supposedly straight guys would lie around naked on the lounge chairs in very suggestive poses. As always, someone would be playing with his dick to get the attention of another. It was always hard to believe the way these guys carried on in broad daylight. I will say this about Travolta: in all my years of going to spas, the sundeck is the only place I did not see him cruising for dick.

George Michael and his boyfriend Kenny Goss used to love the sundeck, often turning it into an orgy of pleasure in the sun. Most times when I would go up there to take in the sun, I would turn right back around and leave because it was so out of hand up there. A ten-man circle jerk was not uncommon to see, with more watching around the corner and masturbating. The place would be completely out of control and sickening.

When I first started going to City Spa, the sundeck was different. You could go up there and get some sun, order a delicious meal from Carlos in the restaurant, relax, and enjoy yourself. That did not last for long. With every passing day, it seemed City Spa was being overtaken by nothing but homosexuals who were having sex everywhere and couldn't care less who was looking or joined in. The sundeck was no exception.

With Jim the masseur having his massage room right off the sundeck, it was like Sodom and Gomorrah. His door was a revolving one, to say the least. As soon as one guy would walk out, another would walk in, eager for one of Jim's final-touch blow jobs.

Eventually, I just stopped going up there at all. It was so embarrassing to be seen coming downstairs because you felt like everyone knew you were just having sex up there.

Oh, and the filth! You would be wise not to tread barefoot up there, but if you did, you had better watch your step. Guys would shoot their load right on the Astroturf and leave it for someone to walk and slip in. Disgusting! Beyond disgusting.

On a few occasions, I mentioned it to Kambiz. "It's out of hand up there."

"Don't go up there, then."

Figures.

I don't know why I bothered. I should have known better than to think he would clean it up. All these gays were paying hundreds of dollars per visit to come to his spa to have sex. He had no interest in stopping it and why would he? They were making him rich.

I took his ill-mannered advice and stopped going to the sundeck altogether.

Chapter 7

CAPPIE

Cappie was a member of City Spa for over fifty years when I met him. Everyone loved Cappie. He was eighty years old at the time and a regular fixture at City Spa.

There he was, on any given day, steaming or in the Jacuzzi. Cappie had made his fortune in life by owning several liquor stores in Pasadena and surrounding areas. He was always interesting to talk to. He had so many stories about City Spa, and he didn't mind sharing them with you.

"In the old days, Al Capone loved the place, and so did many other gangsters. One time, a while back, Kambiz fell into financial trouble, and I bailed him out. He is barely paying me back now. That Kambiz, he's so cheap, he won't even buy me a soda."

"Why do you care?" I asked Cappie. "You've got millions! You don't need Kambiz to buy you a soda or anything else."

"It's the principle. Kambiz borrowed two million dollars to keep City Spa open, and now he can't even buy me a soda?"

Cappie had plenty of stories to tell about Travolta, too.

"I really liked John Travolta twenty-five years ago, when I first met him, but now Travolta's just a sex pig. I don't like being around him anymore. I am not impressed with Travolta's stardom. Over the years, I have seen Travolta disappear into so many rooms with men to have sex, it makes me sick, and I am not even involved! I've heard there is a secret sex tape Kambiz holds over Travolta's head," Cappie said.

It was terrible to see Cappie sad all the time when I'd go to the spa. He never said it, but I would be willing to bet it was from Kambiz's mistreatment of him. I believe he died of a broken heart. Everyone was so sad when Cappie passed away. He was the last of the true old-timers at City Spa. It is a shame Kambiz, the owner, did not treat him with the respect he had earned and deserved.

Chapter 8

CITY SPA RESTAURANT

What a restaurant it was back in the day. Carlos was the cook, and he ran the place for Kambiz. Everyone knew how hard Kambiz was on his employees...especially the Mexicans. He treated them like slaves.

When they would complain, he would insultingly say, "Shut the fuck up, or I'll have you deported back to Mexico, you beaner!"

I witnessed it for myself countless times. One time, after witnessing Kambiz tear into him, I asked Carlos, "Why do you put up with it?"

He said, "I have no other choice. I've got to feed my kids."

He had to put up with Kambiz and his foul mouth. To witness Kambiz in action is shocking to say the least. I would often wonder how one human being could treat another so foul. I never came up with the answer, and that is because there is no reasonable answer for such behavior.

It was not just Carlos the cook who was treated this way either. All the employees knew of Kambiz's rage from firsthand experience. On more than one occasion, I had come upon one of the employees crying, and I would ask what was wrong.

"Kambiz went off on me and said the most horrible things." No one had managed to escape his verbal rampage. It was sad to see him treating struggling illegal aliens so badly.

On any given night, you could go into the restaurant and see it filled with movie and television stars, along with the top athletes and plenty of Hollywood has-beens. Many of Hollywood's biggest deals were negotiated in City Spa Restaurant. On Sundays, all of the powerhouse Russians in L.A. would congregate at the City Spa to steam and you could overhear them discussing business both in the spa and the restaurant..

As soon as you entered the front doors of City Spa, you could smell whatever it was Carlos had prepared for the day. The aroma would lift your spirits and make your stomach growl. In addition, should you so much as take a bite, it was delicious. Every dish that Carlos prepared was always a special treat for anyone's palate.

Apparently, Kambiz had made a deal with Carlos. If he ran the kitchen well, to the point where it returned a profit for City Spa, Kambiz would let Carlos take over the restaurant after five years. Carlos did as agreed, but Kambiz never came through with his promise, even after he had done his part to keep the restaurant operating with a profit for five years. Apparently, you can run a restaurant too well, because Carlos's opportunity would never see the light of day. I seriously doubt that Kambiz had any intention of doing what he had said to begin with. He told Carlos whatever Carlos wanted to hear so that he could play him for five years, knowing that Carlos was holding on and working so hard for the supposed opportunity to one day run his own little restaurant. How sad and cruel of Kambiz.

Despite it all, Carlos was always filled with the best feelings for his diners. He would go out of his way to see to your every need. He had a way about him that made you feel right at home. It was not uncommon to see John Travolta standing at the counter, getting a bite to eat after his massage, and to look over and see Jean-Claude Van Damme eating with his *Entourage* friend, Jeremy Piven, along with John Amos, George Michael, and his boyfriend. Everywhere you looked, stars were eating...some of them half naked! It certainly was a sight to behold.

One of Carlos's best dishes was his chicken soup. I would go to City Spa some days with one thing on my mind, getting a bowl of his soup. It could work wonders on a hangover and zap a cold dead in its tracks. I cannot tell you how many times over the years I have craved and missed his chicken soup.

One night, after I had finished having dinner with John Amos, Carlos came over to talk to me after he saw John leave.

He sat and talked with me for a long time. He said, "You're looking really good, Rob! I cannot believe how much weight you have lost. Milena told me why you are doing it, to meet John Travolta. Rob, John Travolta is a very sick pervert, and if you knew him the way I do, you wouldn't want anything to do with him."

"Why do you say that?" I asked.

"Because I know what I'm talking about. I've known John Travolta for seven years. He's a pervert."

Here it was again, another employee telling me John Travolta was perverted.

Carlos said, "John tried to hook up with me multiple times. I told him I am straight, but that didn't stop John from trying over and over again."

Eager to tell his story, Carlos continued to say, "One time, before I opened the restaurant for business, I decided to take a quick steam. When I got inside the steam room, John was in there with another guy, getting it on."

"Getting it on how?"

"Getting fucked."

I couldn't believe it, another fuck story about John Travolta.

"When I went in, they didn't even bother to stop. They kept at it until I left in utter disgust. I composed myself, got dressed, and went looking for Kambiz. Kambiz told me to mind my own business or I'd be fired and deported. This sexual behavior was a regular thing for John at the spa."

Like everything else I was being told, I would learn that what Carlos was saying was true. He volunteered more information, only this time it was different from what I had heard before.

"One day, Roberto, the employee that was used to set John up in a sex tape sting helped Kambiz install a camera in the massage room, and then he went and had sex with John Travolta in the newly monitored room. They had the whole thing on tape!"

Carlos claimed to have seen the footage, and it was very dirty. According to him, you could tell it was John Travolta in the sex tape, no doubt about it!

Carlos also claimed that Kambiz had blackmailed John for years over that. Knowing how scandalous the sex tape was, one of the employees had sneaked into Kambiz's private office after hours and managed to make a copy of the tape.

"Who?" I had to know.

"It's better that you don't know."

I'm thinking at this time, sex tapes? Steam room fucking? What else could I possibly learn about my movie star, John Travolta? Carlos explained to me the reason he wanted me to know all this. He felt I was a nice guy, and he didn't think I knew what I was getting myself into with John Travolta. Carlos, bless his heart, was trying to get me to open my eyes and see the truth, as he put it. I would like to be able to say I took Carlos's advice, but I did not.

I had to see these things for myself before I would believe it. Fortunately, it would not take long. Not long at all.

One day, when I showed up to City Spa, I went to the restaurant for some soup, but it was closed.

"Where's Carlos?" I asked Kambiz.

"That piece of shit was fired."

I was so sorry for Carlos. What could he have done? He was such a good person and employee. I never got to say good-bye to him, and I wish I could have.

Later, I was told by a fellow steamer that they were there the day Kambiz fired Carlos, and they were appalled at the way Kambiz had spoken to him. As the story went, Kambiz cussed out Carlos and accused him of stealing. He called him a piece of shit and told him to get out. He threw Carlos out on the street and kept kicking him, like a dog, down the street, until Carlos finally ran from his former employer and current attacker.

How sad for Carlos to be treated like nothing in front of everyone. It is shameful, and no one deserves that kind of treatment.

Carlos was one of the first employees to come to my aid after Warren Smith tried to murder me at City Spa.

The first time I saw Carlos after that brutal attack, he walked up to me and said, "Rob, if there's anything I can do to help you, please let me know. I know what you are going through. Warren Smith had tried to attack me as well, shortly before he attacked you."

"What do you mean?"

"Kambiz and all the employees knew about Warren's temper and that he had been a coke addict for years, but Kambiz would still allow Warren to use the spa because he spent money there.

"Rob, the night you were attacked, Kambiz told everyone to never tell anybody what had happened to you in the club, and he erased the surveillance tape that had your attack on it." Carlos told me how Kambiz told everyone I deserved it because I had written him a bad check, and that I was just a fag snooping around in John Travolta's business.

Carlos continued, "John Travolta didn't like you snooping around, so he got Warren to rough you up, but apparently Warren went too far. Before the ambulance arrived, Kambiz had employees get up as much of your blood as possible so it wouldn't look as bad."

I could not believe what I was hearing. Had I been set up by John Travolta? Or was it just a random attack by drug-crazed Warren Smith? I do not know to this day. At the time of the attack, the police looked everywhere for Warren, but he vanished into thin air.

At that time I talked with Carlos, he said, "I won't be working at City Spa for much longer. I can tell Kambiz is getting ready to fire me."

Boy, was he right!

Unfortunately, for me, I did not get Carlos's number, and I didn't know where to find him. When I told the detective working my case what Carlos had said, he tried to speak with him, but Kambiz had already fired him. I guess I will never really know all the details of that horrible night when Warren beat my brains out. Maybe it is better that way.

If I found out John Travolta had something to do with me being attacked and beaten at City Spa, I do not know what I would do. I cannot say that Carlos didn't warn me because he certainly did his best to do so.

Wherever he is, I wish him the best, and I hope he is happy. He deserves to be.

Chapter 9

NATE

It's not that I didn't like Nate. Inversely, I always felt Nate didn't like me. Nate is a huge guy, who stands around six foot seven and weighs approximately 280 solid pounds. He is the first thing you see when you enter the doors at City Spa. Never mind hitting the gym or catching a Laker game. In Nate's spare time, he would chase ambulances and then photograph the victims at the scene. That is what he likes to do when he is not working the front desk at City Spa.

When he is working the desk at City Spa, you had better watch out if you get him upset. I have seen him in action plenty of times over the years, just doing his job, and I can tell you…Nate is one person you do not want to upset. I did my best to stay on Nate's good side, but for some reason, he just seemed cold to me. I tried to warm him up with tips on more than one occasion. That kind of worked. He would be very nice then, but it was always short-lived—that is, until the next tip.

You never know what life has in store for you with people. Today, I owe Nate my life. I think the world of him, and I now know he cares for me as well.

After Nate saved my life, I made sure to tell him how grateful I was every chance I got. On that fateful night when Warren Smith tried to kill me, the last thing I remembered before losing consciousness was Nate bursting through those front doors of City Spa to save me, and save me he did. I will never forget my hero Nate! I wish him all the best anyone can wish someone.

Over the years, and on many occasions, I witnessed Kambiz browbeating Nate. He was so cruel in the way he spoke to him. After all, Nate looked after City Spa as if it were his own. He was the kind of employee any boss would want, and yet, Kambiz treated Nate no better than any of the rest of us—the employees, the customers, and anyone else who crossed his path. He was horrible to everyone.

In all my years at City Spa, I never once heard Nate talk about anyone or gossip behind someone's back. If he had something to say, he would say it right to your face. I tried a few times, in the early years, to get Travolta information out of Nate, but no dice. Whatever Nate saw at City Spa, he did not repeat it to anyone, from what I could see.

Nate is the only person from City Spa that I hope does not hold this book against me. I care what he thinks about me, and the last thing I would ever want to do is hurt him in any way. I hope that I have not. I hope he sees it the way I do. The way I see things at this point in the game is simple—if not me, then who?

Who has a better right to share their story than I? Nate knows how badly Kambiz treated me after my life was threatened at his spa. Nate told me he knew all about it, and how sorry he was for it. So I hope he can see this through my eyes and forgive me if my book hurts him in any way.

I would make it a point to always stop by during the holidays and express my forever gratitude to Nate for saving my life. I would express it with words, and money as well. I have every intention of doing the same with some of the proceeds from this book. My hope is that Nate will be able to quit working for Kambiz at City Spa, if he chooses to, and pursue whatever dream he might be dreaming. Then, and only then, will I feel as though I have repaid my debt to the man who saved my life.

However, Nate is humble, and I know monetary compensation is the furthest thought from his mind. As a matter of fact, he had a hard time taking the holiday money from me when I would attempt to give it to him, so I just threw it on his desk and walked away so he would be forced to pick it up.

He is not a greedy man, nor a Hollywood player. He's Nate, my hero! I appreciate his humbleness, but he saved my life that horrible, horrible night…and I owe him.

Chapter 10

THE MASSEURS

Joseph

Vladimir

Erin

Serge

Viktor

Jim

Chapter 11

JOSEPH

When I first began frequenting City Spa, everyone knew Joseph was Travolta's masseur. It was a title Joseph wore with great pride around the other masseurs, masseuses, and customers as well.

Joseph is a very sweet man who gives a wonderful massage. He is truly a loving human being, who happens to be a wonderful composer who writes from his heart. Therefore, it was Joseph I set my sights on, to get to know him, and to earn his trust.

In return, I would learn all about Travolta. At least that is what was running through my head. I will say this about Joseph: He is not your usual masseur. He really knows how to hold his water and keep his mouth shut. It would take a very long time, and many excellent tips, before Joseph would eventually start to open up and trust me.

During the time I spent with Joseph, when I wanted to learn about Travolta, I was also learning more about Joseph. He started sharing with me his love for music, and once he learned I, too, was a composer, we were like kindred spirits.

Most of the time I spent with Joseph would be comprised of learning a new song he was working on or helping him with lyrics for another one, but most always, it involved Joseph and his music.

Then one day, out of nowhere, as I lay on the massage table, Joseph started speaking about Travolta. Joseph's heart was very heavy. I knew something was troubling him, yet had no idea that it would turn out to be something to do with Travolta. He started my massage and told me that John had moved on.

Joseph was very distraught. "John Travolta will never get another massage from me," he said. in a voice filled with hurt.

I was dying to know what had happened, and all the details, but that is where Joseph left it, but, I never press the issues, never, so I left it at that. However, I could not wait to book my next appointment with Joseph, hoping he might tell me more about what was troubling him.

So, as usual, I gave him a big tip and crossed my fingers that he would remember my generous gesture so that when I saw him in a few days, he would open up to me. Well, it worked! The next time I saw Joseph, he opened up and went on to tell me what had happened. He had asked John Travolta one question, and because of that one question, John Travolta would no longer go to him. My curiosity was peaking, and I just had to know what that question was.

Unfortunately for me, he stopped on that note, and I was out of time. The massage was over.

I pondered the thought, what question could John Travolta's personal masseur of several years ask him that would offend him so much, that he would now be going to Vladimir, another masseur at City Spa? A masseur who had long endured Joseph throwing it in his face that he was Travolta's masseur? Now it was Vladimir's chance to return the favor.

Everyone at the spa knew Joseph was out and Vladimir was in, and it has remained that way till this day, but I'll get to that in a bit.

The next time I saw Joseph, I got to hear the story. One day before a massage, John Travolta said to Joseph, "My rectum is extremely sensitive. I need a lot of work on my hole."

Joseph said he felt offended just by the sound of all this "sensitive hole" talk. For the record, Joseph is Russian, with a thick Russian accent. He looked at me, then said, "Robert, I'm rubbing John like normal on his ass cheek. Then he starts to moaning and moving around...I don't understand this, what he's doing."

Turned out John was lurching toward Joseph's fingers as to maybe have them slip into his gyrating rectum. He could not believe it! John Travolta was in a gyrating, rectum-thrusting craze.

"John, what is wrong with you today?"

"Nothing's wrong with me. My ass just needs a lot of attention."

So Joseph said he thought to himself, *Okay, maybe his ass is sore from too much deep tissue massage.*

Joseph continued, "He started moaning and groaning like I never seen before. He started yelling to me, 'Do your job! Rub my rectum!'"

Joseph went on to tell me how, the whole time, John was thrusting his ass back at Joseph in a very suggestive way. If actions speak louder than words, John's actions were shouting, *"Fuck me, please, Joseph! Just fuck me!"*

Poor Joseph. He said John's moaning was like a deep, wailing moan. Shocked at what he was witnessing, Joseph said he screamed the question, "John, are you gay?"

"Why? Would it matter?" Travolta replied.

"It wouldn't matter, but you must leave your butthole on the table and stop moaning."

Joseph said John stopped cold, got up, and walked out of his massage room, never to return. When the fellow masseurs and masseuses heard of the question Joseph had asked Travolta, they all couldn't wait to tell Joseph how stupid he was for asking him that question. Seems, as they all said, they knew better than to ask John Travolta if he was gay.

As I mentioned earlier, Joseph had been John Travolta's one and only masseur at City Spa for years. But now, because of this infamous question, Joseph had been replaced quicker than the time it took to ask it. Joseph never really recovered from that blow. He always had a sadness to him. He loved the notoriety that came with being John Travolta's one masseur, and all the clout that it brings in the massage world.

One day, while talking, Joseph looked at me and said, "Robert, all I did was ask John if he was gay, and now I'm blacklisted forever."

To Joseph's credit, I would like it to be known Travolta was not the only A-lister he had on his list of clients, but the loss of Travolta as a client just aged poor Joseph. He was not the same.

I felt sorry for Joseph, I did, but I was already planning on how to gracefully dump him so I could move on to Vladimir. Joseph would cry on my shoulder, and my shoulder was always there for him. It was nothing personal, but as soon as I knew Travolta had moved on, I knew I was moving on too.

It was a difficult task switching to Vladimir because it is a very small group of masseurs and masseuses there, and they all know each other's business. To top it off, Vladimir and Joseph's massage rooms were right next to each other. I did not know what I would say to Joseph if he caught me coming or going. I was in a real dilemma, but if Travolta was out of the loop now, there would be nothing more I could learn from Joseph. Remember, I was on a mission here, so I set my sights on Vladimir, the new and exclusive masseur to the one and only movie star John Travolta. I would do just as I had done with Joseph, which was pretty much spend a fortune on massages and tips so he would share all of Travolta's secrets with me—the good stuff only his masseurs would know.

On many occasions, Travolta and I would be booked back-to-back, and on those visits, I always got a wealth of information. There was a rumor that John really left Joseph's service for another reason…supposedly something to do with what was between Vladimir's legs.

What was this I was hearing? They were saying John went to Vladimir instead of Joseph because Vladimir had a huge cock and John loved it. They were also saying that Vladimir was fucking Travolta.

All I can say for sure is that John has never stopped going to Vladimir since he started, and I finally found out why. I saw Vladimir's dick. Oh my God! I have never seen another like it. He belongs in the circus. He is a human oddity. His cock is so huge, it would make a horse's dick pale in comparison. Vladimir looks like a farm animal with that dick. He obviously uses a cock pump. Nobody's dick is that big…nobody's! It is a remarkable sight. I have seen a lot of dicks in my life. I have never ever seen anything like that!

Years and years would pass until, finally, John Travolta gave Joseph another go. He paid Joseph back, dearly, for crossing the line. John blacklisted Joseph for seven years, which goes to show he definitely knows how to hold a grudge. To make it worse for poor Joseph, there was a punishment to go along with it. During that time, when Travolta got a massage from Vladimir, Joseph would know about it, so it stung every single time...for many years. In addition, sometimes Travolta would get two a day from Vladimir! Poor Joseph.

Chapter 12

VLADIMIR

Now, there were two stories circulating around City Spa as to why Joseph was no longer John Travolta's private, exclusive masseur. There was the story that arose from Joseph himself telling everyone how he questioned Travolta about his sexual orientation, and because of that, no more job. It made perfect sense. Everyone who heard the story agreed asking Travolta about his sexuality was enough to dismiss Joseph's services. It was none of Joseph's business, and he had no right to make Travolta uncomfortable with such a question. At the same time, Travolta had no right to make Joseph uncomfortable with his thrusting pelvis and rectum seizure, which prompted Joseph to ask such a question in the first place. It is a line you can be sure Vladimir has not crossed in over a decade as Travolta's exclusive masseur at City Spa.

The other story, or rumor, if you will, was that Vladimir had such a huge cock that John Travolta had fallen in love with it, dumped Joseph, and now only wanted

Vladimir's services. Being a man who appreciates a man who's packin', I was dying to know.

Anyway, this just made everything that much more juicy. Remember Milena? Well she kept adding fuel to the fire. She would say things like, "Oh, baby, everyone says Vladimir's dick is so big that John Travolta is in love with his cock."

She would constantly repeat this, seemingly day after day. I was going crazy with my own thoughts and visualizations.

I dropped Joseph like a hot potato and started having regular massages from Vladimir.

Vladimir's massage is an extremely good one. He really puts his soul into his work, and you can feel it, and no, not just because of who he is and all he told me, but because I truly believe that Vladimir's massage is one of the best in all of Los Angeles.

I always tipped Vladimir forty dollars, and he would be blown away every time. "That's an eighty percent tip," he would say ecstatically. "In all the time of knowing John Travolta, he never gave more than ten dollars." Everyone everywhere has always made comments that confirmed Travolta is very cheap in every way.

When Vladimir told me that, I knew I was "in." Over the years, after many massages and tips, I would learn many things through Vladimir about the great movie star John

Travolta. At this point, Vladimir had been Travolta's masseur for years.

I will never forget the day Joseph caught me leaving Vladimir's after a massage. He looked at me as if I had betrayed him in the worst way. I don't think I did. He was very expensive to hang with, and without him massaging Travolta, he would not have any new news. As nice of a man as he was, he became worthless to me in my quest to meet Travolta, so Vladimir it was…for hundreds and hundreds of tales of Travolta.

Vladimir, more often than not, would be a little drunk. He'd be so sweet and tell me stuff about Travolta. For the most part, the stuff he would tell me would leave me feeling sad for Travolta at some point. After enough stories of visual accounts and the straight truth about Travolta, I felt nothing but true sorrow for him. He was the world's biggest movie star, wallowing in fungus-infested steam rooms throughout the world.

After years of hearing about the real Travolta, I no longer had love for him. I pitied him. I didn't want to change his life anymore and, by this time, gave up all my foolish dreams of being John Travolta's boyfriend. In the beginning, I remember I couldn't believe it was true that John was gay. However, after witnessing his constant and relentless cruising for gay sex, there is no room for doubt in my mind.

Vladimir would go to John's house on many occasions to give him his massage. (Never for more than his ten-dollar tip.) I guess John must have thought it was a privilege and a gift to massage him. A gift? So full of himself. At this point, you know, for a few extra bucks, John Travolta might have made a few more friends. I always say, it is better to have friends than have enemies, but he's always been so cheap with everyone, and he's gotten away with so much. I know the people who run the spas. I know the workers there at City Spa are all going to be happy that the truth is coming out about Travolta. Their poetic justice indeed.

I have always remembered this story Vladimir told me of John. He was very proud as he told me, "John Travolta takes me upstairs to his room and shows me this little box, and inside it was the most beautiful diamond ring I had ever seen, and it was for Princess Diana's birthday."

I remember down the road, months later, reading about the ring John Travolta gifted to Princess Diana. It confirmed what I already knew about Vladimir, that being, the information I learned from Vladimir did not come cheap. I always found it really interesting how the better the tip, the better the insider info would be the following time.

Sometimes I would get five massages a week. Those weeks I would learn a lot about Travolta. Vladimir made many claims to me that his children were conceived through artificial insemination. He would tell me this story again and again. Vladimir told me about this one time, after a two-hour massage at John's Brentwood home, John had been drinking a little wine and started to get emotional. He told Vladimir that he and Kelly could not conceive the traditional way, because John could not get his penis erect.

Vladimir disclosed how John had cried, saying he was a failure as a husband, and a fraud. The conversation made Vladimir uncomfortable, so he said.

Now, after seeing Travolta and learning all I did from Milena, Joseph, and Vladimir, the rumor I believe to be the truth was the rumor that John Travolta stopped getting massages from Joseph flat out once he saw Vladimir's cock. I wholeheartedly believe John went insane for it. If you could see it, it truly is the largest, most sexually enticing cock I have ever seen. Trust me, if you could see Vladimir's dick, you'd know I'm right, too.

For the most part, the picture I got from Vladimir was that John Travolta is a very lonely, sexually confused person, to be pitied, not envied. All things considered, Vladimir had known him long enough by that point that I think it's fair to say he knew him really well. There would be no trading Vladimir in for the next masseur, because Vladimir is still, to this day, very proud to let you know John Travolta is just one of his many celebrity clients who now wait for appointments with him.

When Vladimir is massaging you, he gets really into it. At first, I felt uncomfortable because this guy grinds his body on yours as he's massaging you, and at the same time, he is making all the sounds that imitate someone having sex.

But I soon learned this was just his way. A way that Travolta apparently likes.

One day, during one of my many massages from Vladimir, I asked him, "What do you think about the way Travolta cruises for sex and hooks up in the spa?"

Vladimir said he knew about John's "sexcapades," and that the owner, Kambiz, had told all the employees to look the other way should they see Travolta hooking up in the spa. Vladimir went on to say John is a very sick man who is like an alcoholic with sex. He just couldn't stop, and Vladimir feared the worst for Travolta—that he would be caught sucking some guy's dick in a corner of the spa by an undercover cop.

Chapter 13

ERIN

Everyone would agree, Erin was one of the nicest guys you could ever meet. He sure was a wealth of knowledge for me regarding John Travolta. The first thing Erin said to me when I met him in the early nineties was that I looked a lot like Travolta…except that I was the better-looking one!

Well, of course, from the get-go, I loved Erin. I would book massages with Erin on Vladimir's days off so Vladimir would not find out and get all mad at me. These masseurs get very territorial over their clients, and the last thing I wanted to do was upset Vladimir, John Travolta's number one masseur. From the very start, Erin held nothing back about Travolta's antics at City Spa. At this point, Erin had been at the spa for years and years. He shared so many stories about John's spa hookups that it made my head spin.

Erin said, "In the early nineties, Kambiz caught John upstairs in one of the empty massage rooms having anal intercourse with a City Spa employee named Roberto. John had been after this Roberto for a long time, and he finally got him to fuck him. While it was going down, in walks Kambiz. It was all a setup by Kambiz so that he could blackmail Travolta."

Erin claimed that all the employees knew what Kambiz had done to John.

"Shortly after Kambiz caught John in the act, he supposedly blackmailed John into giving him money to keep the spa going. In addition, along with that, Kambiz assured John that from then on, he could use City Spa as his own personal whorehouse so he would never be bothered again. It was shocking to hear," Erin continued.

"John set Roberto up in his own place, and was never seen again at City Spa after that fateful, premeditated night. John would continue utilizing City Spa as his own house of sin with no end in sight. John became so much more brazen after being caught."

He shook his head.

"John Travolta is a very lonely man. I believe he has a sex addiction. I feel sorry for John. I've been witnessing John's shocking behavior for years. With every year, he gets more perverted and takes more risks at the spa. John gets massages from me on a regular basis. He is a horrible tipper. He never gave me more than my usual ten-dollar tip. It is no secret to me that John Travolta is gay. He would always request 'ass-work' done, and after years and years of massaging John Travolta's asshole, I got tired of it. Every time, he got weirder and weirder. I just prefer not to work on him anymore."

I could tell Erin cared about him when he explained how Hollywood had turned John into a sex addict and a very unhappy man.

I always enjoyed my time with Erin. He had such a gentle way about him, and he gave a good massage as well. Not to mention, he never disappointed me when it came to Travolta.

On one of my last massages with Erin, he told me that he was no longer giving massages to John Travolta.

With my curiosity piqued, I asked, "Why not?"

Erin explained, "The last time I was rubbing John's ass, he asked me to do something so filthy that I refuse to repeat it."

Of course, I tried to pry it out of him, but Erin would not budge. All he would say was that he would never touch John again as long as he lived. No matter how much the tip was. From his facial expressions and body movements, it was obvious he was upset. I wondered what it could have been. Did John ask Erin to fuck him?

Erin knew of Milena's scheme to make me into John Travolta's boyfriend. He also saw all I did to transform myself. He was always so encouraging about it. I can still hear him saying to me, "When you get him, you won't want him, because he's sick. He's an addict for sex in the worst way. Rob, you're dreaming. It's all fun to dream about it, but

John Travolta is never going to settle down with you or anybody. Due to his sexual drive, wants, and desires, he's simply not capable of it."

Erin sure knew what he was talking about.

There was another thing that bothered Erin regarding Travolta's massage appointments with him. Erin said John showed up with about fifty to a hundred wigs and hairpieces that he would put on in front of Erin and ask him his opinion. Travolta, for some reason, valued Erin's hair choices for him. Erin said John was beyond obsessed with his hair loss, and he shared with John what he knew about the Bosley hair company. Apparently, Erin booked the VIP appointment for Travolta and even met with him at City Spa on the day of the consultation at Bosley's, then rode with him to the appointment. The bottom line was John's hair was too far gone for surgery, and wigs were all that were true options for him. Erin went on to say that while they were on their way back to City Spa after leaving the consultation, Travolta started crying really hard, saying his hair loss was unfair and why him, why a movie star. Erin said it was pathetic to see him so vain. This was not the first time I had been told about Travolta's hair obsession. He pestered Vladimir, Joseph, Viktor, and all the male masseurs on a regular basis. They, too, were victims of the "which hairpiece do you like best" game. According to the masseurs, they all said Travolta could not accept the fact that he was going bald.

Did John ask Erin to fuck him? Was it true Travolta could not accept the fact that he was going bald? Well, I will never know, because he never told me, and because, I am sorry to say, Erin has since passed away. He was a very nice man, and I know he is in a good place. His presence was missed at City Spa after his passing, and he continues to be missed to this very day.

Chapter 14

SERGE

From the moment I met Serge, I knew he was not going to be easy to get to open up, so I went extremely slow with him. Milena had told me it was going to be hard with Serge. She said he was really tight-lipped and he didn't even talk with his fellow City Spa masseurs.

Serge is a really big Russian with huge hands. He talks with a heavy accent similar to that of Vladimir's. His presence is intimidating to most people who see him, but he is really a sweet man when you get to know him. That is what I did for a very long time before we got to any of the Travolta escapades. I took my time getting to know him. After about two months of weekly massages and big tips, he finally started to open up about his life at the spa.

I have never heard Serge say one bad thing about anyone, except John Travolta. And when it came to Travolta, watch out! Wow! Serge couldn't stand "John the Pervert," as he called him.

"John walks around the spa masturbating, and I'm sick of seeing it. He should be in jail for his behavior inside the spa, but Kambiz has made it all possible for him. John would never talk about his son, Jett, when I would ask him. John was ashamed of his son, and everybody knew it,," Serge told me.

When I tried to be coy and ask him about Travolta, he had a mouthful to say. "Rob, it's no secret what you're up to. Everybody who works at the spa has heard about Milena's scheme with you to get John Travolta. Milena was only using you for the money. If you want to meet John Travolta, you don't need Milena's help. You can do that on your own."

He was genuinely concerned about me dealing with Milena. Serge did not like her, and he certainly did not trust her. I listened to his words of wisdom, and I had a strong feeling he was right.

In addition, he was! Everything he said back then turned out to be true.

He went on to offer, "If there's something about Travolta you want to know, just ask me, and, if I know, I'll tell you."

He was the only one from City Spa who made my quest to get close to Travolta easier for me without putting a dollar amount on it. He wasn't after my money.

With a voice of disgust, he would ask me time and time again, "Travolta is a filthy, filthy pig. What do you want with a pig?"

So one day, I asked, "Why do you say Travolta is a filthy, filthy pig?"

"Because he is. I have seen it for myself. Everyone at City Spa knows that John Travolta is a closet homosexual who leads a double life at the spa. Every employee at the spa has caught John in the act of lewd sex acts many times. We all joke about it between ourselves."

I guess he was in the mood to hand out advice as well. "Rob, you don't have to remake yourself for Travolta. I have seen John hook up with more fat and ugly old trolls than anything else. The only thing that man cares about is getting some dick. It is common knowledge that he likes to catch, not pitch. That is, he likes to be fucked. Most of the times when he's been caught in the act, he is being fucked. We all call him John the Pervert behind the scenes."

Serge claimed to have seen Travolta masturbating to orgasm more times than he cared to count, and that John didn't even care who might walk in and see. Serge told me there was an employee named Oscar who Travolta was trying to woo with money but, so far, Oscar had held out. I wonder how long he held out for.

A story that sticks with me is the one where Serge said he was giving Travolta a massage, and John told him he needed his ass rubbed real good. He had already heard about this before, so Serge was prepared.

"I'm not a proctologist, and I'm not rubbing your asshole. And one last thing, I'm not giving you massages any longer," Serge notified John.

"If you don't give me the massage, you'll be fired."

"If you get me fired, I'll go to the tabloids and tell them the reason I got fired was for not finger-fucking the great John Travolta in his ass."

Apparently, after that, John left Serge completely alone. Serge could not have been happier.

Chapter 15

VIKTOR

Viktor gave a great massage and an even better blow job. He did not have to ask twice if I wanted full release or not.

"Yes, please!"

He had dark features and was very handsome. I had heard he was very thorough with his massage and he knew how to use that mouth for more than talking. And, as it turned out, it was all wonderfully true. I have such great memories of Viktor. He was a cool guy, and there were no extra charges for the full release. Everyone liked him. He knew everybody's business in City Spa, and he loved to gossip.

He, like his fellow masseur coworker, Jim, and superstar John Travolta, used City Spa for his own personal sexual escapades. He'd be the first to proclaim what a whore he was. And no one was more celebrity starstruck when it came to sexual encounters than he was.

Viktor would announce, "I've been keeping a journal since I started working here. Someday, I'm going to publish it."

It never ceased to amaze me. I used to think, back then, how nobody would believe all that goes on inside City Spa; the hidden Sodom and Gomorrah of today is right here in L.A.

Viktor would brag often, "Me and John Travolta have been hooking up for years." After Viktor would massage John, they would have full-blown anal sex in Viktor's massage room. "John was truly a bottom who loved to get fucked. The nastier the sex, the more John liked it. I really liked sticking it to Mr. Movie Star."

Milena had told Viktor of her plan for me and John from the get-go, and Viktor would offer his opinion from time to time. "I think you could be the one to tame John Travolta."

Viktor was always telling me when John would be at the spa so I could get there and spy on him. It was exciting! I was becoming an insider to a world I had only just discovered by chance. Viktor went on to say that all the masseuses were talking about the latest ban on Travolta from a spa. This time it was Burke Williams that had banned Travolta from ever returning to their facility. He said the number of spas that had banned Travolta had grown to more than 30 facilities on the west coast alone.

One day I pulled up to the spa, and all the employees were talking about Viktor getting fired. Seemed he, too, pushed the limits, and had gotten himself into a lot of trouble for having sex with a minor in the spa. I never saw him there again.

Years later, I would run into him at a function, and we talked. He pretty much said what I had already heard, and that was that he had fucked up. He asked me if I had ever landed Mr. Movie Star, and what had I been up to.

It was nice to see him. I told him about the book I was writing about City Spa. He said he wanted the first copy and that I had better use his real name. He is so funny, and I wish him the best. I'm sure we'll talk again.

Chapter 16

JIM

Jim claims to have blown Travolta when he first started working at City Spa.

I don't know that for sure, but what I do know is that Jim would become an overflowing source of information about City Spa and, most importantly, John Travolta. Jim would share the lurid details about every celebrity and customer he would give his famous City Spa blow job to.

Jim would boast that there were hundreds of dicks that had touched his lips while working at City Spa for the past several years. He always said he loved his job at City Spa because he didn't have to go anywhere else but to work to get all the dick he needed. The fact that it was celebrity dick made Jim that much happier, so he said.

Jim was also very well known at City Spa as a drug dealer. He sold Vicodin and cocaine on a daily basis and had a lot of side rackets going on while he was employed at City Spa. One such racket he was proud to let me in on was that he had been making money for years selling stories to the tabloids of what he saw at City Spa.

Jim had no problem smiling in your face and then stabbing you in the back as soon as you walked away. That was just Jim.

I liked him when I first met him. I knew a backstabbing person like him could help me with my objective to learn as much as I could about Travolta. All it would take was money, and since I had plenty of that, a friendship was born.

Jim's massage room was located right off the sundeck on the second floor, where everyone would lounge out for sun, and the ones wanting more than just sunshine, well, they would fondle their penises to get whomever's attention. With Jim's massage room located where it was, and with Jim always lurking around so willing to accommodate, he always had great stories of his latest victims he had deceived. Jim was definitely the most ruthless, hard-core, noncaring human being I met in all my years at City Spa, besides Kambiz, the owner.

When I asked him if he would help me in my pursuit of Travolta, a resounding "definitely" was his answer.

Jim told me he had had a conversation with Travolta about Scientology. He was giving John a massage, and asked him one question about the church. John, he said, did not stop talking about Scientology until the massage was through.

John revealed to Jim how the Church of Scientology had been blackmailing him ever since he first started going there. "After I did all my auditing at Scientology, they used the recordings to blackmail me into promoting the church. I have been trying for years to get away from them, but so far, I have not succeeded. They are evil. They are a cult."

Jim sold that story to one of the tabloids shortly after John shared it with him. Jim also thought it would be a good idea for me to experience Scientology for myself, so I would have more in common with Travolta. Therefore, in the spring of 1998, I made an appointment at the Celebrity Center on Gower, to go find out for myself about this Scientology thing…but more about the Church of Scientology later.

Jim was always calling me to tell me if Travolta had been at the spa, or if he had seen Travolta hook up with anyone. Of course, with Jim, everything came with a price. He made a bundle on me, but I wanted to learn as much as I could about Travolta, so it all seemed worth it. Quite often when I would get to the spa and go up to Jim's massage room to see him, he would be finishing a drug deal. It was not uncommon for me to see Jim selling eight balls of cocaine right along with his grandmother's prescription.

"I was at my grandmother's house today, and I stole her Vicodin. If you want to buy any, let me know."

I remember thinking, *How low can you go? Stealing your grandmother's Vicodin and then selling it.* However, that was just Jim.

I had to get at least two massages a week from Jim in order to keep him flowing with info. If I did not, he would hold back on me. He was always very business driven. Everything equaled money to Jim.

On one of my very first massages with Jim, I felt a sudden warmth, and when I opened my eyes, I couldn't believe it! He had the head of my penis in his mouth.

He paused and said, "It'll be great. Trust me, some of the biggest celebrities in Hollywood have had this mouth."

I thought to myself, Travolta has had it, and all these other VIPs have had it, why not?

As soon as I let him know it was okay, he looked up, released the suction from my dick, and said, "It's going to be thirty dollars more on top of the massage."

I said all right. He locked his lips around my dick and commenced giving me Jim's famous City Spa blow job. A guy knows immediately if it's going to be good or not. Let me tell you, in all frankness…he knew nothing about sucking a cock.

While he was bobbing up and down, doing his thing, I was thinking, *This is what has Travolta coming back for more? If it is, then Travolta, and all the rest, can keep him and his blow job.*

I lay there thinking, *How am I going to get out of this?*

No time to think, because out of nowhere, he stuck his dick in my face. I was in complete shock and told him so. "Jim, I'm not into this."

He was very pushy. I couldn't believe the way he was acting! He kept trying to stick his dick in my mouth. I couldn't stop him from trying, so I just got up.

"I'll still give you the thirty bucks, but it's just not working out."

"Oh, well, you don't have to pay me. Let's just suck each other off."

The thought was making me sicker by the second, not to mention he has this real ugly birthmark all over his penis, and it is not pretty. I walked out. I didn't care if he wasn't going to share more of Travolta's spa antics with me or not. I was getting out of there.

Being true to who Jim is, he wasn't going to let our little escapade stop him from working me for money with Travolta calls and stories.

Jim eventually was fired from City Spa for having sex with one of his customer's sons. Apparently, he gave the son a massage, then pulled the same move he had pulled on me and started sucking the kid's dick. The son freaked and ran to his father. He told his father everything, and Jim was escorted off the premises.

I heard that the kid's father filed a lawsuit against the spa that was settled out of court. Jim is now selling real estate in L.A. Someone I know went to an open house, and as fate would have it, it was Jim's listing. My friend said that when he went into the house, it was very quiet, and moments later, they heard a guy having an orgasm in the upstairs bedroom.

Then, Jim and some guy came out of the bedroom as if Jim had been showing the house. But, as usual, Jim was blowing, not showing, the prospective buyer of the house.

Some things never change!

Chapter 17

TRAVOLTA JOURNAL ENTRY
April 29, 1997

So here I am, sitting in the parking lot of 7-Eleven.

I just left City Spa. *Oh my God!*. I ran smack-dab into my future boyfriend, John Travolta. I was going to head over to see my grandmother after I got off work today, but I had a hunch to go to City Spa instead.

When I arrived there, I did my search of the parking lot to see if I could see any of Travolta's cars so I would know if he was in there or not. If I see his car, I always leave, as Milena said no meeting Travolta till she says so. Well I hope she does not hold this against me.

When I checked out the parking lot for his cars, I did not see any of them, so I thought it was okay to go in and use the treadmill, followed by a steam. I made my way past the entrance, said hello to Simon when he buzzed me into the spa, and right smack-dab in front of me was John Travolta coming out of the restaurant.

Our eyes met, and he said, "Hello, how are you?"

Oh my God! John Travolta just flirted with me. I can't wait to tell Milena. Anyway, we just looked at each other and smiled. Thank God, I checked my look before I went into the spa. I looked cute today, and I was fully dressed, so Travolta couldn't tell what my body looks like.

Thank you, God! I can't believe I've spoken to him before my makeover is complete. Shit, there was nothing I could do about it at this point. I looked up and *bam!* He was right in my face. I am glad I ran into him even if Milena gets pissed. After all, it was the universe that made it happen for me. I needed this. It has given me renewed motivation with my makeover to be Travolta's perfect boyfriend.

Next thing I knew he was gone; he exited toward the steam room. I stood there and watched him disappear into the steam, as much as I wanted to go sit next to him in the steam room and tell him I have a crush on him. I know how whack that sounds, and I'm still revamping myself. I knew I had to get out of there. There was no steam for me today. I went to the front desk and told Simon I had to leave immediately for a family emergency that came up. I wasn't about to stay in the spa and get into trouble with Milena. She will be glad I left. That way Travolta only got a glimpse of me, and then I vanished.

I love it!

When I got to the parking lot, I saw his car. I don't know how I missed it. He is driving that blue Rolls Royce today, and it sticks out like a sore thumb. It is gaudy! I wonder why he likes that old queen's car. First thing I will have him do is get himself a sexier car that looks more like him.

Last time I saw him, he was driving his 1992 white Mercedes SL500. It is certainly a better look than the Rolls. Today has been over the top!

I spoke my first words to John Travolta, and he acted very taken with me. I know we'll be together. I can just feel it!

It is only a matter of time before I will be done with this whole makeover plan. Then, I'll be free to really know this amazing person. He is so much cuter in person. I'm going to head over to my grandmother's house, as I had originally intended.

Chapter 18

PRINCESS DIANA
August 31, 1997

Growing up, I heard people everywhere say they remember exactly where they were when President John F. Kennedy was killed. My mother knew where she was, and so did my father. They would talk about it as we were growing up. I was only a few years old, so there's no way I could remember that terrible tragedy, but I sure know where I was when I heard Princess Diana had just died.

I was at City Spa, and like millions, I was floored with the news. I had just finished a full day at the spa, so I was in the locker room getting ready to take off. As always, the TV was on.

They interrupted the show that was on to report the news of a horrific accident involving a car that Princess Diana was in. The report came across that it was a terrible one and possibly fatal.

"We're standing by, live, and should have more for you in just a few minutes," said the newscaster.

"She can't die. She's going to be fine," I said to myself.

The spa had become silent. The normal clanging of locker doors and the unmistakable sound of flip-flops had come to a halt. The news spread like wildfire, and everyone was rushing into the locker room to see for themselves.

Carlos the cook, all the masseuses, everyone. We all stood there watching the TV in suspense, when all of a sudden the broadcaster said, "Oh my God, this just in…Princess Diana died just moments ago."

The broadcaster was losing it.

I was losing it.

Everyone around me at City Spa was losing it.

It was heart wrenching to say the least. I had to sit down. I was in complete shock. Hearing the news that Princess Diana was, indeed, dead felt like I had just heard my own mother had died. It was that leveling. I sat there on the leather couch in shock and did not budge for at least an hour. As I sat there, the rest of the world was slowly becoming glued to its TV, too. With every passing minute, more people were hearing it, and a dulling sadness overcame even the toughest of people.

This news, in a strange but wonderful way, brought us all together worldwide. We were all united in the grieving and loss of the beautiful and adored Princess Diana. The world resounded with praise, commending her for the tireless deeds she did for so many, saying how she truly had the heart of Mother Teresa. Is it any wonder they both died within days of each other? Two pure, loving souls going home to God. "They did so much for so many," was what everyone was saying. Days after her death, Diana's long list of charity work was continuously compiling. She really was a saint on Earth.

We all knew we lost someone very special and that loss would tear through the fabric of people across the globe. I can't imagine a place in the civilized world that wasn't talking about Princess Diana, and I was no exception.

When finally leaving the spa and heading home that fateful day, I drove home in a fog, an absolute fog. Princess Diana was dead, and she was never coming back. Period. As surprising as it was for me to experience this unexpected loss for someone I had never really kept up with, I knew it was a true loss that I was somehow connected with. People all over the world were speaking out and saying that her death had left them blindsided. They could not explain it, because many of them, like me, weren't really fans prior to her death. Nevertheless, after her passing, they became loving, adoring, mourning fans who will always remember where they were the day Princess Diana passed away.

Staying up to watch the funeral was not an easy task. I was just a wreck. Bawling my eyes out, I had reached out to God and asked of him, "Why did you take her and leave me? She was worth so much more to the planet." That's just how

I felt. As impossible as it is, if I could have traded my life for hers, without question, I would have. That is how hard her death hit me.

I had never been a royal watcher. I knew of Princess Diana, and years earlier, I had watched her televised wedding to Prince Charles. Of course, in the tabloids, she was always ever present, but I just wasn't a fan. That is, until her death.

It was so touching to learn of all the beautiful deeds she did for people that no one even knew about. It was so touching the world stood still for a moment, and you could feel it.

I will never forget that horrible day and the unbelievable loss the world suffered. I'll also never forget where I was, a place that would, in the end, hold so many memories for me—good, bad, and indifferent. City Spa.

Chapter 19

SCIENTOLOGY

While revamping myself for Travolta, I knew the time would come when I would have to learn more about his faith, this thing called Scientology. I had heard so much about it, and if John Travolta was into it, I knew I at least had to do my homework.

Around 1998, I made an appointment at the Celebrity Center near Gower in Los Angeles. When I arrived for my appointment, I walked into the building and down the hall. The first thing I noticed was a picture of John Travolta and his wife Kelly Preston. It was of the two of them standing together and was placed on a credenza inside one of the offices.

By the time I left the Scientology Celebrity Center interview that day, I had learned a wealth of information. After a while, I lied and told the woman interviewing me I was friends with Travolta, and that he and I belonged to the same gym. When she heard I knew him, she immediately told me how she'd always wanted to meet John, and that, in all the years she had been there, she had never seen nor met

John Travolta. In the photo on the credenza, he was wearing a red blazer. Red sports coats were really cool in the late nineties. I had one as well.

I must have seen that same photo no less than thirty times that day. Everywhere you looked, there were John and Kelly posing like a married couple. However, in reality, things were not shared between them like there would have been if they had the true intimacy of a married couple. There is a facade for the world to see, and it only benefits them as far as I can see.

The interviewer would gush whenever I would bring up John Travolta's name. I thought it was weird, if he was so involved, that this woman who held a high-ranking position in Scientology would be so star struck with Travolta. That's because she had never met him, nor was she around him. If she were, she'd be done with the star struck bit!

So the fact that John Travolta's picture was everywhere at the Scientology center was an enlightenment to me. He's always quoted giving praise to the Church of Scientology, and yet he's apparently never there. Hmmmmmmm!

The whole time this woman was interviewing me, she asked me personal things about Travolta, like, "What's he like in person?"

Like everything I had witnessed about Travolta, I could see this whole Scientology thing was also a facade. It was very surreal. I even went through all their required testing and examinations.

That day, they even had me watch this film. In addition, at the end of the film, the narrator says, "Without Scientology, there is no hope for anything."

What about God? I thought. What a crock of shit! The Scientology they were selling in 1998 was so full of itself. I couldn't help but think how sad it must be for people to be so lost that they have turned to the words of a deceased out-of-work actor, L. Ron Hubbard, and his Dianetics bullshit for guidance. How ironic is it that a huge part of the Scientology following are people who wanted to be actors? These individuals are filled to the brim with severe insecurities.

The pictures of John Travolta and Kelly everywhere throughout the Celebrity Center—in the hall, in the interview rooms, in the theater, and even in the gift shop—began to ring a bell and make sense. They were placed everywhere strategically!

I let her finish the interview, and I promised her I would bring Travolta over one day to meet her. It was so weird. I wanted to tell her, *"Why don't you just shut up? You're sitting in front of a picture of John Travolta and his wife, and you're acting like he's single or like you don't know the truth!"* She was acting like an utter moron. I was hoping that I would have a better understanding into Scientology after my appointment, and I most certainly did!

Now here is what I found out about John and the Church of Scientology. One of the masseurs told me that when John Travolta was just getting started in the seventies, Scientology was a hip alternative to modern religion. Now, when John joined, he went through hours and hours of auditing. The head of Scientology has held that audit over him for all these years and used it to blackmail him. In John's youth, he told the auditors his most intimate and personal thoughts, as well as his desires, and they have been pulling the strings ever since!

I was also told, once you are a member of the Church of Scientology, and they have audited you, *they own you.*

A source told me John had no choice but to stay and endorse the Church of Scientology due to his fear of the truth about his homosexuality coming out.

He was told point-blank, "If you leave the church of Scientology, we will make sure the truth about your sexuality is revealed to the entire world."

As a result of the threat, he has stayed. John Travolta lives with so much fear and loneliness from all the addicted sexual dysfunction his life brings him.

I was also warned that if I wrote about Scientology, I'd be killed. We will see about that! I am only writing what I was told by those who know the truth. I learned many things at the Scientology center that day that saddened me, but the most saddening thing was all these vulnerable people were being charged astronomical amounts of money to feel accepted.

The whole premise was sickening. It left me feeling so glad I had my relationship with God on such solid ground. As always, God is there for all of us. He is free; he doesn't charge a cent!

While feeling pity for the lost souls who ended up at the center, I also felt great joy in knowing I knew the difference and the truth. It was another look into the fabricated movie star life, the old-school style, when you had to hide who you really were because no one would accept you for being gay.

John Travolta wasn't an active member. He was instead, as I'd been told years earlier, a puppet on a string. I was also informed that when all those reports came out about Travolta from his boyfriend, Paul Barresi, the Scientologists helped to arrange and put together John Travolta's marriage in an effort to do damage control for his reputation. They scratch his back; he scratches theirs. He is in bed with Scientology—that's for sure!

How deep or how far, only he and Scientology truly know. Any road that leads to God is a great road, and is the road for you. There wasn't the slightest evidence or presence of God anywhere at the Scientology Celebrity Center I visited. I felt elated when I left there. Their prediction for doom and gloom was only that, a prediction, and a false one at that. Maybe there is a purpose for the Church of

Scientology after all, because I felt more connected with my own beliefs after visiting that Celebrity Center that day than I had in a long time.

I made an appointment to return to the center with my hefty down payment and to start my new life, as they put it. Of course, by then, I knew I had seen all I needed to see. I also knew the woman who interviewed me was sent from God because she was the right one at the right time, providing me with a source of information I couldn't have possibly attained otherwise. Now that is God's work! I could read between the lines and knew all along I would never be returning to that dreadful place again. I didn't have a clue at the time that I'd be writing about it someday. Wow! Now here I am telling my story.

As I drove away from the Celebrity Center that day, I was in deep thought. What a bunch of users and losers! Those Scientologists who prey on the weak may have healthy bank accounts, but they are morally piss-poor. It's all very frightening, and I, for one, want to stay as far away as humanly possible from that production over there.

Chapter 20

TRAVOLTA ENCOUNTER
June 5, 2000

John Travolta is about to have a new child, his second. Her name is going to be Ella. It also happens to be the day that Milena says is my day to meet John Travolta.

I couldn't believe it had taken five years to revamp myself to meet Travolta. By now I was smoking hot. I'd lost seventy-five pounds, I'd followed Milena's advice to the T, and, now, the culmination had arrived. I have to say, at that moment in time, I was truly at my best in so many ways. I had never looked so hot!

I had achieved the unattainable goal, and as promised, I was going to get my movie star, John Travolta. What I didn't know back then was by the time I got there, I wouldn't want John Travolta at all. He wasn't, by any stretch of the imagination, the person I thought I was looking forward to meeting. He was there, nonetheless, and so was I.

So Milena called me and said, "Get over here, baby. Today is the day! Travolta is coming in for a massage with Vladimir at six o'clock. You be here at five o'clock sharp.

He'll be at the spa early, before the massage, to watch dick."
That's exactly how she said it.

I arrived at the spa, got undressed, showered, then
went to the pool and prepared my naked, toned, perfected
body to dive into the pool. Just as I made my jump, I glanced
over, and like a dream, John was standing there, looking, and
lusting, for me, just like Milena said he would. I watched
John's eyes go from my torso to my now dangling penis, and
then I hit the water.

I knew he'd be standing there when I came up for air,
and he was. He approached me and immediately introduced
himself. My heart was in my throat. He told me he was
having a child soon and that they hadn't released the gender
yet to the media. So he tells me it's a girl and they are going
to call her Ella. We carried our talk over into the Rock Room.
Every person in there stood to shake John Travolta's hand,
all ass-kissy, and as soon as he walked out, every single one
of those hypocrites mocked him.

I couldn't believe what I was seeing again. Just a
minute ago, in John Travolta's presence, they were kissing
his ass. Then as soon as he walked out of the Rock Room to
cool down, this asshole poked fun at John as the other spa
members joined in. That's just so typical of Hollywood. Just
pure bullshit!

I felt sorry for John because he was so full of himself.
It was to the point where he couldn't even tell who his

friends were or weren't. As long as they kissed his ass, he loved it.

After I left the steam room, John was gone. I immediately ran to the phone booth in the locker room. It was the old-fashioned kind with the closing door, like the one Clark Kent uses to change into Superman. I nearly dropped the coins I had in my hand, overly anxious to call my mom and tell her I'd finally met John Travolta. Right then, John passed by the phone booth as he came in to get ready for a massage. He looked over at me on the phone as if I were calling the tabloids about the baby's birth or something.

It was a very uncomfortable moment when our eyes met. I wanted to open the phone booth door and tell him, *"I'm trying to call my mother to tell her I've met you."* But I didn't.

I swear, the look he gave me was that of disgust, anger, and rage rolled up into one. From his standpoint, I'm sure he was thinking, once again, someone was selling him out. It's unfortunate, after all the effort and time put into meeting John Travolta, it would go down this way. I now knew in my heart of hearts that Travolta was not the guy for me. Now getting away from him and his constant sexual advances towards me would take years and years. Every year, I'd witness his behavior that led me to pity his lonely life and his sad way of creeping around.

Chapter 21

MILENA

Looking back on everything now, I can see how naive I was with Milena. However, if I had to do it over again, I would. It was an exciting time for me. My life was filled with so much potential, and my dreams were becoming realities, and Milena guided me every bit of the way.

We had so many adventures. And those adventures are the reason why we became very close. We were spending almost every day together, and with every day came more Hollywood drama.

Milena made it a point to introduce me to every star who came through City Spa's door. She claimed no matter how persistently she tried to give John Travolta a massage, he would never let her touch him.

"Everyone knows John does not like females touching him," she would explain. But, for some reason, she was not going to rest until she showed John Travolta what he was missing.

As far as massages go, he was missing a lot. To this day, I've never experienced a better massage than Milena's.

John Amos told me, in his opinion, she was the world's best masseuse, and I agree. In the beginning, I was just a guy following a rumor about Travolta, and now I found myself deep in Travolta country, with all the collateral damage that came with it. An example of this would be, the more I worked out, lost weight, and got closer to my goal of meeting Travolta, the more Milena would complain about her own physical appearance and financial hardships.

On a moment's notice, Milena would call me. "I need to borrow two thousand dollars because my mother in Russia needs emergency brain surgery."

"Who is doing the surgery?" I inquired sarcastically. "A veterinarian?"

Needless to say, I gave her the money. I knew she would never repay me. The roller-coaster ride with Milena was definitely more than I had bargained for while on my quest to meet John Travolta, but it was too late. The train had left the station!

It seemed the more I got myself together, the more self-conscious Milena seemed to become. When it came to Milena's concerns with her physical appearance, her teeth seemed to be of dire importance. Now that I had capped my teeth to meet John, she felt especially ugly. Well, I'll give her that! She was right. That woman needed a lot more than capping her teeth to make her look pretty.

Milena mentioned how she wanted her teeth capped too, as she said, "Oh, baby, I'm helping you to land John

Travolta. Can't you please make my teeth pretty, too? I would feel embarrassed talking to Travolta about you because my teeth are so ugly."

Feeling the pressure of her request, I gave in and bought her a full set of beautifully capped teeth, hoping to keep the mastermind behind my meeting John Travolta happy.

I should have known that soon after I was done with my dermatologist, she'd suddenly feel too ugly again to talk to Travolta about me until she got the full treatment: heavy-duty laser sessions—I think there were five of them—and Botox everywhere you can possibly put Botox. Of course, she needed fillers in her lips and face, as well. All in all, the trip to the dermatologist set me back another fifteen thousand. I thought to myself many times, *Isn't it me that is supposed to get made over here, not you,* but it seemed she had other plans. As I've said before, I was so naive when I first met Milena, and so filled with stars in my eyes for John Travolta, that she most definitely was able to play me like a fiddle.

I was thankful when I was finally done with my entire makeover treatment. I didn't know how much more I could afford with Milena constantly nagging me for her share. In the end, Milena didn't look much better. She just didn't. She would have been better off doing something more drastic, like a major face-lift. At least that way she might have had a chance at being pretty. Instead, she just highlighted all that was wrong with her face...and let me tell you, there was plenty.

I decided if I was going to do anything else to improve my appearance, I would not tell Milena. Then, my only outpouring of money to her would be in way of massages and tips. At least I knew from experience that I would come away from it with plenty of Travolta talk and the latest secrets of the celebrity clients she saw and worked on at the spa. This cut my expenses considerably.

Just before the millennium came in 2000, I thought it would be great to bring in the New Year at the Chateau Marmont in West Hollywood. It had been a favorite hotel of mine for years, and I wanted to be there for New Year's Eve...so did Milena.

This would turn out to be the beginning of the end of our common-goaled relationship. By the time New Year's came around, I was basking in the glory of greatness. I had reached my weight goal, my beautifully toned body was ripped, my teeth, with all their perfect caps on them, were stunning, absolutely stunning, and everyone everywhere said so. I was flying high, to say the least.

I invited a bunch of friends to my suite for cocktails before we all headed out for a night of celebration and partying on the Sunset Strip. When Milena showed up around seven to the Chateau Marmont, she was the first to arrive, and in a very foul mood.

"What's wrong?" I asked.

"I just found out my Cadillac Escalade is going to be repossessed in a few days." She was hysterically crying. "Oh my God, baby, what am I going to do without my car for work?" she said with tears rolling down her face.

I knew what Milena was doing, but I also knew I didn't want her ruining my New Year's Eve millennium party, so I said, "Oh, you poor thing! How much is it going to cost to save your car?"

"Twenty-five hundred dollars," she quickly replied.

"Wow! That much?"

"Yes," she went on, "I've been helping you so much with this John Travolta scheme that I've been forgetting to pay my car payments."

Inside my head, I was laughing hysterically. But I simply responded with, "I know you have, sweetie, so I'm going to help you with your car." I asked her, "If I give you the money right now, would you feel better and be able to be in a more festive mood when my guests arrive?"

"Oh, yes, baby!" she said with a cat-that-swallowed-the-canary smile.

I went to the lobby and withdrew $2,500 from my safe-deposit box and took it back up to the suite.

As soon as I walked in, she screamed out, "Did you get it, baby!"

"Yes."

She was happy for the moment, thank God! I figured this would be the last time I'd let her play me, with my introduction to Travolta behind me now. If I had kept track of how much money Milena got from me during that time, I'm sure the amount would be staggering.

Guests started arriving, and the room was filled with excitement over the arrival of the millennium. I had no clue I'd be back in my suite alone by 12:30 a.m., ringing in the New Year without anyone.

Everyone was talking about what was going to happen to all the computers in the world—would they shut down or keep going? There were rumors that the military computers might malfunction and fire nuclear weapons at other countries, causing a domino effect, leading to a world war. People ran out in droves purchasing survival gear, including sardines, bottled water, and gas masks. Well, I'm happy to say the millennium came and went without any catastrophic drama, but for me, the drama would start just before midnight…with Milena.

I'd never seen Milena drunk. I was witnessing a wild woman. She turned into a complete mess. She was screaming at everyone, saying that I was John Travolta's boyfriend, that she had made it all happen, and that I was now going to run off with Travolta and dump her.

Well, I didn't know about the Travolta part, but I was definitely going to be dumping her. She went on to tell everyone there all I had gone through in the past several years pursuing Travolta, even elaborating about how I was so fat when I first met her that she didn't have the heart to tell me, and that John Travolta didn't like my type. She was now saying things completely different from before. Like I said, I had never seen her drunk. What an eye-opener for me! This New Year's Eve was an epiphany on many levels.

I remembered what Serge had told me a long time ago about Milena and her lies. I decided that it was over. She kept talking to anyone who would listen about my Travolta quest. It was embarrassing, but at the same time, it was freeing. I could see Milena for who she was so clearly now, and I couldn't stand what I saw.

The first chance I got, I ditched Milena at the club. It was ten minutes till midnight, and I was walking alone down Sunset Boulevard, back to the Chateau Marmont. This was not how I thought New Year's Eve would progress, but I was thrilled to be finally free of Milena.

While it did take some time for her to get the hint, she eventually did. She apologized many times for her behavior that night, but it was too late. This was supposed to be about Travolta, not Milena. I made up my mind that I was done with Milena's help. I was exhausted with all her antics and was completely through with her at this point. For me, I'd seen and had enough of my BFF Milena. Her final words to me back then were that she couldn't pay me back the money she had borrowed...as if I ever thought she would!

It had been five long years of revamping myself in order to meet John Travolta, and now that it had come, I no longer wanted him for myself as I had in the beginning. I'd seen and heard too much about who John Travolta really was.

I knew my heart held no more than pity for the movie star.

There were no more stars in my eyes, or anywhere else for that matter.

I was seeing John Travolta for what he truly was: a lying, deceiving homosexual who didn't have the balls to come out of the closet. Back in the beginning, I thought all John Travolta needed was to meet a nice guy and he would be happy.

Not the real John!

The real John is only looking for sex with as many people as he can find. The way he deceives his fans is terrible.

To witness the famous John Travolta for yourself, you would be truly shocked that he's gotten away with such lewd behavior for so long. The fact that he continues to deny his homosexuality, and then goes and puts on live sex shows at public spas, is disgusting.

He's nothing like I thought he was going to be. Instead, I discovered a complete and utter fraud. Everything he says is self-serving. By this time it was confirmed that I hadn't needed Milena to meet John Travolta. All I needed was my big dick, as was made evident by what I'd witnessed hundreds of times in the past with Travolta's lovers. It was a lot of fun, though, spying on John Travolta and getting close to his personal masseuses to find out all about his personal life they had witnessed, and everything that came with my years at City Spa.

Chapter 22

TRAVOLTA ENCOUNTER
June 29, 2003

It had been one day since I purchased the one-year memberships at City Spa, one for myself, and the other two for my two closest friends. I called them to tell them the good news about me purchasing their one-year memberships at the spa, and to meet me there later that day. I was excited to give them their membership cards, so Nate hurried up the process and gave them to me early so I could give them to my buddies when they arrived. My friends were ecstatic over their gifts. I wanted to have them enjoy the ritual of steaming, and besides, it's nice to have a friend with you when you're sitting in the steam room. It can make the time go by so much faster.

As planned, they met me in City Spa's parking lot. They were right on time. I gave them their memberships, and we went in. I introduced them at the front desk and showed them around. They were wide-eyed and excited to be members. After the tour, we went to the locker room to get ready to go steam and relax. We decided to shower and then sit in the Jacuzzi for a while.

Once in the Jacuzzi, I closed my eyes for a minute, when all of a sudden, one my friends said, "Oh my God, there's John Travolta over there masturbating."

I opened my eyes, and I couldn't believe it! There was Travolta, with a fully erect cock, stroking it and staring right at us. He seemed to be focusing his glare toward my two beautiful friends who were in their twenties and had the bodies of Adonis himself.

My other friend said, with a shocked look on his face, "Look at him. He's staring right at me as he's jacking off!"

I had told them both for years about Travolta's antics at the spa, but I guess they really had to see it for themselves.

"You've been telling us the truth about Travolta all along, Rob."

This wasn't news to me!

I have to say I was taken by surprise with Travolta on this day. I had long since put away my silly dream of making him happy as his boyfriend, so his lewd behavior was no longer my concern. I hadn't even been thinking about him on this particular day. I was enjoying being with my friends.

All three of us sat there in the Jacuzzi and watched Travolta choking his chicken while licking his tongue in and out in a wild sex frenzy. Kind of reminded me of an episode of *National Geographic* about snakes and why they dart their tongue in and out. Snakes are always on the prowl, and so was the infamous Travolta. It really made my very straight friends absolutely sick.

"I've seen enough! Let's get out of here!" They literally leaped out of the Jacuzzi.

So we got out and headed to the pool to cool down. Of course, that pervert was fast on my friends' tails. It wasn't me he was after; it was this fresh young meat I had brought with me to the spa. They couldn't stop talking about how shocked they were, and how ugly and fat Travolta was.

"He's fucking bald, too." They burst into laughter.

We stayed in the pool while Travolta stood close by, licking his lips and continuing his reptile impersonation for what seemed like forever, when suddenly Travolta made a gesture to my friend to follow him to the steam room.

To my surprise, my friend said, "I'm going to go and see what he tries to do with me."

My other friend and I just looked at each other in surprise. So he headed into the steam room, where Travolta was waiting for him. He claims that when he went in, Travolta was masturbating and said to him, "Did you like what you saw when I was showering?"

My friend told Travolta, "Well, it certainly surprised me!"

Travolta asked my friend to sit next to him so they could talk. My friend said he obliged Travolta, and as soon as he sat down, Travolta grabbed my buddy's dick. He claims he only let Travolta hold it for a minute, but I have to tell you, they were in there for a lot longer than a few minutes. After the interlude in the steam room was finished, Travolta hurried out and showered, and was gone in a flash.

To this day, I'm sure that my buddy hooked up with Travolta, even though he's not gay. I've seen plenty of straight guys turn gay for the moment with Travolta, so he was having a gay moment. He still claims nothing further than touching happened. He mentioned many times how big Travolta's dick was, and if Travolta ever got tired of traditional movies, he could certainly be a porn star. I've heard that one a million times as well. Everyone who has ever seen Travolta's cock has always commented on how big his package is.

We ended the day with a meal in City Spa Restaurant. I couldn't help but think what a perfect day at the spa it had been, including the movie star pervert. It couldn't have played out better if I had written it myself.

It didn't take long before both of my new City Spa co-member friends were calling to tell me what they saw Travolta doing at the spa. Every other day, it was another story of what they had witnessed. Old news to me, breaking news to them. Eventually, it became old news to them, too, and they wouldn't even bother repeating the latest sexcapades they had observed. In the end, they both thought of Travolta as a pervert, and someone to be pitied, not admired.

One year is all they were able to stand of seeing such lewd behavior, with all that went on in City Spa. When it came time to renew their memberships a year later, they declined to do so.

Chapter 23

THE BEATING!

It was October 25, 2003. It was a real gloomy day that had turned into an even gloomier night. When I got to City Spa, I desperately needed my steam. It was, to say the least, a very hard time in my life, and now, tonight, someone was going to try to kill me...and almost succeed. It's a miracle I'm alive. That's what they tell me, and that's what I know.

On this night, I saw Warren Smith, and right away, I could tell he was on one! By "on one," I mean you could tell he was out of his mind. You could always tell with Warren, so I stayed the fuck away from him. My senses would be on overdrive. I would not take my eyes off of him. The minute I would see him coming, I'd dodge out of the way or wait in the dark for him to pass.

This night, though I gave it my best to avoid him, he saw me. When he looked at me, his eyes peered into mine, saying, *"I'm going to kill you!"*

So I got the fuck out of there.

I threw on my clothes, paid my bill, and said good-bye to Nate at the front desk. Minutes earlier, I had seen Warren putting metal blocks into a sock, which would later become the instrument created out of his insanity to kill me, and it almost worked.

As I walked out the front door, Nate said, as he always did, "Be careful out there."

What I didn't know was that Warren was already waiting for me behind the front entrance door.

As I walked out, a voice from inside my head shouted, *Turn around!* and I did just in time to somewhat break Warren Smith's blows to my head. If God had not warned me, the doctors said those first blows would have laid me out and I would have never known what hit me, but instead I fought.

I fought for dear life, and I screamed in bloody horror, "*Nate! Nate! Nate!*"

All I remember is there was this kid sitting right there at this bus stop, watching me being beaten almost to death, and he did nothing to help me. *Nothing!*

I remember feeling the blood from my skull run into my eyes, the result of multiple continuous, direct, and deliberate blows intended to end my life. He continued and continued until, all of a sudden, shock must have set in. Because even though he was still beating and beating me, I now felt numb.

All of a sudden, a voice said, *You're dying now,* and I remember feeling absolute peace. I felt no fear. It no longer hurt. At the last possible minute, Nate burst through the front door of City Spa, and Warren bolted from the scene.

I kept coming in and out of consciousness. I think mostly I was fighting the urge to go to sleep. I knew I had to try to stay conscious, but I couldn't, and the very last thing I saw was Nate laying me in the lobby of the entrance to City Spa—my beloved spa for so many years—and I remember thinking, *Look at all my blood.* The whole entrance was a pool consisting of my limp body and what seemed like gallons of my own blood.

I heard Nate desperately calling 911 over and over again. He so wonderfully spoke to me, saying, "Hang on. Help is coming."

I would soon thereafter be comatose.

He was sent from God. If it weren't for Nate, Warren would have gotten away with his murder attempt, and no one ever would have known my attacker was someone who used to be a friend of mine from the spa, who was now a coke addict and my possible murderer…and that would have been that.

Chapter 24

CENTURY SPA

Century Spa came into my life when I could take no more of John Travolta at City Spa. I was still a member there, but running into John all the time was just too much. After all I had gone through with my transformation from head to toe, and spending thousands on massages to gather information about him, only to discover the real Travolta and to know he's not at all who I was told or thought he was, after all that work, I just had to find another spa, so Century Spa it was.

If I'd go to City Spa and one of John Travolta's cars was there, or if I thought I saw his body in the house, I'd simply leave and head to Century Spa, where I wouldn't have to deal with his cruising. It was a spa to go to so I didn't have to run into John Travolta anymore. *Wrong!*

By the time I first ran into him at Century Spa, I had already purchased a membership and was getting to see the same type of City Spa behavior reenacted here at Century Spa. Just shameful! Unfortunately for me at this point, I had no idea Mr. Travolta was a regular at Century Spa as well. It didn't take long to find out, because soon I was running into him at Century Spa all the time. By no stretch of the imagination was Century Spa anything like my beloved City Spa where I felt there was a feeling of family there.

Century Spa is family owned, yet there are terrible things I've seen and been told of by employees. The family consists of the mom and pop, plus their son, and I quickly found out this Korean spa likes to keep it a family operation.

I've witnessed the mother speaking terribly to American customers, telling them to get out. She has been both nice to me and a bitch to me over the years. That woman has a very nasty tongue on her. For all I know, it's forked!

Then there is her homosexual son Edward who uses the family spa as his own personal whorehouse. I've known him personally for years. Not only does he take advantage of the business his family owns and operates, but he's a ruthless individual. He'd stab his own father in the back, if someone hadn't already beat him to it.

Edward is creepy, like you need to be concerned creepy. He runs through those steam rooms every few minutes, checking out all the men. Edward pursued me from day one. He would see me coming into the spa, and in minutes he'd be in the sauna talking to me. He was always leaving me notes on my car. I just wasn't into him. I let him know right off the bat I wasn't interested in him as a boyfriend, but we could be friends, but that didn't stop him from pursuing me.

Over the years, I watched Edward go from an in-the-closet homosexual to a flaming, cock-crazy, penis-hunting spa owner. The most shocking thing I saw (and heard from many) is that Edward has all the rooms set up with cameras and recorders, and uses the footage for personal enjoyment and profit. Out of all the spas in L.A., Century Spa is the place to cruise for lewdness. I've witnessed more filth there than anyone could possibly believe. Oh, and let's not talk about athlete's foot. Oh my God, the worst!

One day I was robbed, along with other Century Spa members. A bunch of lockers were broken into by a thief whose description was a dead ringer for Jeff Kathrein, and all Edward and his mom said was, "We're not responsible for your stuff. Not our problem."

Everyone who knows Edward and his family spa co-owners knows how rude they are to Americans, and I hope now some of those guys will think twice before becoming free porno for Edward's discretion.

Lastly, Edward's father was stabbed to death by his employee, who claimed he was being robbed of his tips. The father just laughed it off, as the story goes, so the employee murdered him at the spa. It's a place I'm glad I'll never see again.

Edward did share with me a few things. He told me all about Travolta's current antics at his spa. Back when all the lockers were broken into and I was robbed, Edward was showing me footage of the entrance to the spa. The footage suddenly cut to the steam room and locker room areas, where video cameras were off-limits, by law, for privacy concerns. Before I could get a good look at who was on the video, Edward was in a panic to keep me from seeing anything. He frantically tried to find a way to stop the footage, but had to resort to turning the monitor off in haste. He looked back at me, hoping I hadn't seen what I saw…but I had, and it was someone in one of the massage rooms getting his dick sucked by another guy. It was an awkward moment for Edward, the owner of Century Spa, but for me, it was confirmation that there were cameras everywhere, some for Edward's personal pleasure.

Chapter 25

TRAVOLTA ENCOUNTER
July 15, 2006

I swear to God, if I didn't know any better, I'd swear John Travolta was stalking me. It was July 15, 2006. I had just arrived at Century Spa, and I couldn't wait to get a great steam in.

Oh no, there's Travolta's white Mercedes SL500 in the parking lot. Not again!

I was faced with the decision of either staying and trying to enjoy my steam while avoiding Mr. Movie Star carrying on like a deranged cock hunter, or leaving to avoid Travolta at all costs. Could I stomach witnessing his antics while I steamed, or should I just go back home? I reasoned with myself that since I was writing a book about his secret spa life, I might as well take advantage of another chance to observe how the world's most famous movie star spends his free time, so I headed on in.

Bingo!

The Koreans really go gaga over him whenever he visits the spa. I hadn't even made my way completely through the entrance before one of the employees, Mai Ling, shouted out, "Oh my God, John Travolta is inside!"

"Really?" I said, as condescending as ever.

She looked like she might faint. There had been so many times when I'd seen Travolta slide into a spa and go seemingly unnoticed. That certainly was not the case that day.

Once I got in, I could see that it was jam-packed, and everyone was after Travolta. I spotted him immediately. He was headed into the dry sauna. He was at full arousal and had quite a following. He didn't stay in there long before heading to the shower, where he put on a show for all to see.

First, he lathered up his penis with soap and started stroking it. There were no less than fifteen guys watching him, including the owner's son, Edward. One guy walked up to Travolta and started talking to him. All the while Travolta continued to stroke his own manhood. Clearly, the guy was trying to get him to follow him to the more private rooms in the back. As usual, Travolta obliged, and they sauntered into the dark room. The group of star struck sexual deviants were hot on their tail.

When John came out of the room, he was ready to leave. He had so many guys after him by now that it became uncomfortable for him. He never liked crowds of people to be at the spa when he was there, so he got ready to leave, but not before taking a shower and giving everyone another full-blown XXX shower show.

His dick looked especially big when he emerged from the dark room with that guy. I never could figure out how he always got away with his lewd behavior, and in front of so many people! The word "disgusting" is not strong enough to describe his actions at the spa, and "pervert" does equally as much justice describing him as an individual.

Why does he continually put himself in these risky situations? He must be dying to get caught, just like George Michael, Tiger Woods, and Jesse James. They all put themselves at risk, and so does he.

After Travolta got dressed and headed for the exit, I noticed the guy he had hooked up with ran up to him and gave him his number. I watched Travolta head out to his car, and along the way, I saw him toss the guy's number in the trash. After he drove off, I went over to the trash can and picked it out. Sure enough, it said: *You were amazing. Please call me*, his name and number neatly printed next to the message.

Silly fool, I could have saved him the trouble with that one. *Mr. Travolta isn't looking for love; he's looking for rock-hard, throbbing, ass-probing dick.* I just laughed thinking that silly gay boy actually thought he had a chance to do more, or be more than a boy toy, to Travolta. When I finally went back in to steam, the entire spa was buzzing about Travolta's big dick.

There were a few straight guys I overheard talking in the steam room. In particular, this one guy said he was appalled by what he saw John Travolta doing, and that he was never going to see his movies again. The poor guy was in shock, and well, who wouldn't be?

I asked him what had happened, as if I hadn't seen, and he said John Travolta had just jerked off practically in front of everyone in the spa. He went on to elaborate, "I have never seen such filthy behavior before. My wife is never going to believe this one!"

Trust me, it is pretty unbelievable…until you see it with your own eyes.

Chapter 26

MY STOLEN WATCH
January 11, 2006

John Travolta's boyfriend stole my watch. At least that's what I told the police and everyone else I spoke to about the theft at Century Spa. The long-running rumor was that Jeff Kathrein was John Travolta's boyfriend, and he also doubled as Jett Travolta's nanny.

All I know is that when I arrived at Century Spa on January 1, 2006, Jeff was there in the locker room, acting very strange. As soon as I came in, he started staring at me, so much so that it made me uncomfortable. I noticed him watching my every move. He didn't take his eyes off me. I kept wondering where his boyfriend, John Travolta, was.

They were always together, but not that particular day. Apparently, Jeff was cruising for sex without his famous boyfriend in tow. At least that's how it appeared to me. He was staring at me like a guy does when he wants to hook up. Remember those old cartoons where Wile E. Coyote would be gazing at the Road Runner, only the Road Runner appeared to be a big, juicy hot dog? If you remember, you know exactly how I felt.

I hadn't even had a chance to get undressed, and this guy was all over me with his eyes. He repulsed me. He was acting like a tweaking, cock-crazy spa whore, and I wanted nothing to do with him. I mean, I was really offended with his pushy sexual demeanor. I let him know of my disgust by turning my back to him while I got undressed. This pervert wasn't getting a free show of my dick.

The last thing I did before I closed my locker was remove my Rolex watch that I had recently purchased to the tune of $11,000. Just as I took it off, I couldn't help but notice Travolta's boyfriend making sexual gestures toward me as though he wanted to suck my dick. I set the watch down and closed my locker door.

As I walked past Jeff, he looked at me and said, "Hey buddy, want to play?"

I stopped, looked at him, and said, "No thanks."

What nerve this guy had! The moment I got into the showers, I told my friend who was with me what had happened in the locker room with John Travolta's boyfriend. He told me, "Jeff Kathrein comes to the spa a lot without John. He's just as big a whore as John. He's a top, and he's very aggressive with everyone he encounters."

"I know that firsthand now, because he just practically raped me with his eyes in the locker room while I undressed."

(For those of you who might not know, a top is someone who provides the dick, and a bottom is someone who accepts it.)

After finishing up my shower, I went and got in the Jacuzzi. From where I sat, I could see the door to the locker room, and the door had a window. Through that window I could see Jeff Kathrein staring at all the naked men from inside the locker room. His actions were very bold, yet odd. He was either scoping some cock to wrap his lips around or he was casing the joint for a future burglary.

Five minutes later, suddenly, a Korean member comes running through the locker room, saying he had been robbed. "You better go and check your lockers!" he shouted.

I couldn't believe it, and as soon as I got into the locker room, the Korean guy said, "I saw this white guy running out of the locker room." The description he gave perfectly matched Jeff Kathrein's.

Once I opened up my locker, I saw I had been robbed as well. My beautiful watch was gone, along with my wallet and my money, and John Travolta's boyfriend, Jeff Kathrein, did it.

Here I thought this pervert was watching my every move when I arrived because he wanted to hook up with me, when all along, he was casing me and planning on robbing me, along with many others. In total, seven people were robbed that day, and every one of them gave the same description of the mysterious white guy they saw in the locker room. They just didn't know he was John Travolta's boyfriend, but I did. I'd seen them together for years now. It was no secret.

When the police came, I told them exactly who I thought had robbed me, and they were shocked. Edward, the owner's son, was no help to the members who were robbed in his spa either. That day, as usual, Edward was too concerned about himself to have anyone else's interests at heart. He and I went over the surveillance tape that morning, and you could see John Travolta's boyfriend enter the spa. Unfortunately for me and the seven other victims, I did not know Jeff's name at the time, so that didn't help much. But I would later learn, without a doubt, it was Jeff Kathrein.

The police took the burglary report and told me a detective would be in touch. As my luck would have it, I never heard from the detectives about the theft. So, in the end, it ended up being a total loss for me.

Why would Jeff Kathrein be breaking into lockers? His boyfriend is rich. Over and over again, that very question would pop into my head.

I gave up trying to figure out why people do the strange things they do a long time ago. Only he knows why he was acting out like that and why he robbed me and the other members that day instead of doing what he usually does...have sex at the spa. One thing I know without question is John Travolta's boyfriend stole my watch!

Chapter 27

TRAVOLTA ENCOUNTER
December 16, 2006

Today is December 16, 2006, and I just got done putting away the manuscript to *You'll Never Spa In This Town Again*. I spent hours writing all the Travolta stories I remembered last night. I was blown away by some of the memories I recounted. Most were very vivid, as if they had just happened recently. I wrote a lot last night, and then I found myself writing earlier tonight as well. I believe the universe gives you signs, so I put away my manuscript and headed over to Century Spa to steam and shower.

On the way over, I thought about my book, City Spa, John Travolta, and when I would ever see him again. I parked my car and headed into the spa. I made my way into the locker room, and lo and behold, I saw John Travolta sitting on the couch. I couldn't believe my eyes.

He looked up at me as I walked in pretending not to see him. So, I passed right by him on my way to the locker room, and I could see him watching me through a reflection in a mirror. Standing there at my locker, with my back to him, I felt paralyzed. And couldn't move. Utter shock had overcome me because here I was, writing about Travolta's lewd behavior at City Spa, and here he was, up to his tricks at Century Spa.

I walked away from my locker, passed Travolta, and I shuddered to his voice saying, "Hello Rob." He was still seated on the sofa, pretending to read magazines, although he was flipping pages a hundred miles per hour.

Stuck like a truck in quicksand, I had no choice but to say hello while simultaneously telling myself to be strong. He wished me a Merry Christmas, and I told him the same. It was extremely difficult to look Travolta in the eyes, and not because I was ashamed, but because I was embarrassed for him. Here I was writing about Travolta being out of control, with his brazen style of cruising for cock in the spas, and in front of me is the famous actor, John Travolta, looking like a heroin addict waiting for his fix at a different spa. John's look on his face is one of someone who is lost and can't be found until he gets a lot of cock. We exchanged holiday pleasantries as I progressed out of the men's locker room. I decided not to shower, and as I walked, I watched Travolta in the mirror. Sure enough, he was watching me leave.

It felt as though he knew I was writing a book about him, but I knew he didn't. I get in my car and pull around to the front so I could watch John when he came out. There he was, sitting on a bench outside, talking to this really short guy named Michael, who everyone knew had a huge cock.

Travolta obviously knew this too. It was obvious they weren't talking about the Lakers, if you know what I mean. Travolta must have just discovered Michael was packing when he was naked in front of him a little bit ago.

Watching Travolta in action was like perversion in motion. He didn't stop staring at Michael's cock the entire time they were talking. Travolta was licking his lips as he looked at Michael's swollen cock, like a hyena going in for the kill. Michael appeared to be quite pleased to be talking to John Travolta. He kept pulling at his penis through his pants to adjust it more than a couple of times. Travolta seemed to almost faint, as he was locked into a lusty, cock-staring frenzy. Then it hit me. I reminisced on how I once really thought he could change his ways and that we could be closer than just spa buddies, but some addictions are so strong, they will run your life.

I can say from the first time I met John Travolta at City Spa well over a decade ago, he hadn't changed at all. He was as cock crazy as always. I saw another guy come walking up to John Travolta, and they talked for a minute. John ended up leaving with the whore whose name I didn't know.

I heard tires screeching up the ramp, and it was Michael, the little guy with the really large dick who was talking to Travolta earlier. He came roaring through the parking lot, stopped, and looked at me as if, for a second, he thought I was Travolta.

Realizing I wasn't John, he shouted, "Where is John? Did you see where he went?"

I just shook my head, indicating I didn't know where John had gone. He sped out of the parking lot like a crazed lunatic. You could hear his engine roaring from blocks away. What he wanted, I have no clue.

It's sad that John is still so lonely. When our eyes met earlier, I could feel his loneliness, as I always could. I could only hope, someday, that he would be at peace with this addiction of his, the penis addiction that makes him put himself in risky situations, as George Michael did. Tonight, as I watched the second man approach John Travolta on the bench, I had a strong feeling that John's behavior was so out of control that he was begging to be caught. It was so terribly sad for me to watch and witness it all firsthand. At that moment, I felt my heart break for John, as it had so many times before, because I knew there was nothing I could do to stop him. I couldn't change him. With a broken heart, I drove home with a real sense of loss, as if my friend was missing and I had realized he was gone forever.

The John Travolta I loved and cared for had reduced himself to nothing more than a sex-crazed spa whore who was utterly out of control. Poor Kelly, poor Jett, and poor Ella. They deserve better, but until John Travolta gets help, there is no hope for him. His life is filled with days and nights of constant and relentless penis pursuit. Merry Christmas, John Travolta!

Chapter 28

JOHN TRAVOLTA
January 30, 2007

I went to Century Spa around twelve thirty in the afternoon. I did my regular workout and proceeded to the locker room to change out of my clothes, go steam, and sit in the Jacuzzi. As I made my way toward the steam room, the first thing I saw was John Travolta. I was completely shocked. I had never seen him out that early cruising for dick. He was next to Bill, a good-looking Korean guy I know. Travolta's side was facing me, so he was unable to see me when I came in. I scurried by, took a shower, and breezed right past him so he wouldn't see me.

I wanted to take the opportunity to observe him without him knowing I was there. We had known each other for years as City Spa members. What he didn't know was that I'm writing a book about him and his lurid spa activities. The spa wasn't busy at all. Pretty much dead. Besides myself, there was only John Travolta and Bill in there.

I made my way toward the sauna without Travolta noticing me. For the first time ever, the sauna had a light bulb out, so I was able to sit in the corner without anyone knowing I was there. This, in itself, was weird yet fortunate…The sauna was never dark. I sat and watched Travolta in the other room through the glass that divided the sauna from the Jacuzzi.

Travolta was staring at Bill's crotch the whole time, licking his chops the way a Rottweiler does when he's near a bitch in heat. Every time Bill would look away from Travolta, Travolta would grab his own dick and stroke it while the guy wasn't looking. He seemed oblivious to everything except for Bill. I sat there in utter amazement. In front of me, in broad daylight, more or less, was one of the world's mega movie stars carrying on in a sex-crazed, cock-hungry, and horny manner.

No matter how many times I spied on Travolta over the years, it never ceased to amaze me that he was so audacious and cavalier with his behavior, especially since he continuously denied his homosexuality.

Travolta looked exceptionally awful. He was really heavy and had lost most of his hair, a far cry from the movie star depicted in the movies. That day, he looked like your average middle-aged pervert, doing things I'm sure his wife Kelly would be shocked to even know of, much less see. For the first time ever, I noticed Travolta was not wearing his wedding ring. Shocker! Because usually, he paraded his wedding ring as if it were a married-and-straight proof of certification. Just try to find a picture of John Travolta without it on. It would be difficult at best.

It's a very sad thing to see John Travolta so woeful and cruising for sex in public spas. While I was in the sauna, Travolta glanced my way every now and then, but I was sure he didn't see me at all. He wouldn't be so bold...or would he?

I didn't know, but at that moment, it appeared there was only one person Travolta was interested in, and he was sitting right next to him. Bill was a professional masseur who advertised in *Frontiers* magazine. He was a very nice guy. I had spoken to him over the years, and he was definitely gay, but when he came to the spa, he was like me: he was there to use the spa for its intended purpose, not cruise for sex, like Travolta.

I continued to watch Travolta lust after Bill and could see how he didn't appear to be interested. He obviously knew whom he was talking to, but he got up, walked out, and headed toward the showers. Travolta was in hot pursuit. I jockeyed for a vantage point allowing me, once again, to see but not be seen. As Bill showered, Travolta made his approach and stood right in front of him. He attempted to start up a conversation—about what I have no idea.

By Bill's body language, I could see that he was getting uncomfortable with Travolta's forward advances, so he then headed over toward the sauna, where I was. I watched Travolta watch Bill walk away like the hawk who had missed out on the rabbit in the field. Bill came into the sauna, sat down next to me, and we exchanged our hellos. Just then, Travolta came wobbling toward the sauna and opened his towel to reveal his fully erect penis for Bill (and anyone else) to see through the glass window.

At this point, Bill went from being uncomfortable to having a sickening feeling of shock and disgust. He got up and left the sauna and headed toward the steaming area. Travolta, now in full stalking mode, was hot on Bill's tail. My vantage point was lost as they both disappeared into the steam. I have to say I'd witnessed Travolta pull this move repeatedly over the years. Usually it seemed to work, but not this time!

I'd never seen Travolta look so fat, so bald, and so…different. Even his penis looked much smaller now that it was surrounded by layers of fat. Surprisingly, for a celebrity, he didn't seem to care about his appearance at all.

I sat there in the sauna, in a bit of shock myself from Travolta's towel disrobe. As I sat there, I thought about what I had thought so many times…*I should have a camera with me so I can get his picture when he's exposing himself.* My closest friend, Chuck, who knows I'm writing this book, had been after me for quite a while to get a camera and keep it in my car, so next time I ran into Travolta out whoring around, I could capture it on film. I'd like to say I followed Chuck's advice, but I didn't.

So, once again, Travolta was cruising around, showing anyone who would look at his erect dick, and I still didn't have a camera. At this point, I saw Bill exit the steam room he and Travolta had been in. He took a super-quick shower and headed for the exit.

Travolta soon thereafter exited the steam room and headed to the sauna I was sitting in. When he entered, he was shocked to see me in there. We said our hellos.

"Rob, I didn't see you. When did you get here?"

"Just now."

Obviously, he didn't know I had been observing him earlier, and we made small talk.

"I like your goatee. I almost didn't recognize you."

"How's Vladimir doing?"

"He's doing well."

We talked about City Spa. He asked me how my beautiful cock was doing..

"Great," I replied.

Right then, he opened up his towel and started stroking his cock in front of me. I have to say, the vibe was a bit eerie. "Awkward" would be an understatement. There I was observing him, and now he was in the sauna with me and hitting on me again.. A few minutes went by, when Mr. Cho, one of the masseurs at Century Spa, opened the door to the sauna and called out a locker number. It was Travolta's, so he exited the sauna with Mr. Cho for his massage. I knew from past massages it would take about forty-five minutes.

Mr. Cho started working on Travolta right there next to the sauna and steam room, on a table behind a heavy curtain.

I started thinking. *I can get dressed, hurry across the street to Rite-Aid drugstore, get a camera, hurry back to the spa, get undressed, and try to catch Travolta in the act of his nasty behavior.* So I took off on my mission impossible.

Once back at the spa, I undressed, wrapped a towel around my waist, and swooped up a hand towel to conceal my camera while making my way to the massage area where Travolta and Mr. Cho were. As I got closer, I could hear Travolta moaning with pleasure, so I pulled back the curtain just a bit to get a better view. There was Travolta, lying on his stomach, with his huge ass up in the air, moving it up and down in a rhythmic, gyrating motion. He was really enjoying himself.

The temptation to pull the curtain all the way back and take pictures was overwhelming, but I just couldn't. I was concerned that Travolta would hear the camera, see me, and then he'd be on to me, so I waited and listened. His masseur was finishing up. I took the opportunity to go into the sauna with the glass window partition and get myself situated so when he came out, I could take the pictures. I stood there poised and waiting for what seemed like an eternity.

While waiting, I was trying to keep the camera from getting hot in the sauna. Every few minutes, I'd hear Travolta sound off with moans of pleasure from his massage. Every five minutes or so, I'd look in on him and his big ass still gyrating up in the air. I couldn't wait until those two were done so I could snap those candid photos, but as fate would have it, just before Travolta's massage was finished, three gay guys came into the sauna.

I knew from past experiences with Travolta, when there were a lot of people around, he left the spa. Knowing this, I got dressed and headed for the exit. As I was leaving the locker room, I could see him staring through a window, watching the guys get undressed.

He is such a warped individual. I went to my car and moved it closer to the entrance so I could at least get a picture of him leaving the spa. As I waited, this green Dodge Dakota truck pulled up, and the guy driving it looked like this guy who had robbed a bunch of the lockers at Century Spa. A couple of weeks earlier, my locker had been robbed clean, including my $11,000 Rolex. So, for a minute, I forgot about Travolta and focused on this guy, thinking he was the one who had robbed me and others at the spa. I watched him closely. He appeared to go around to the passenger's side and open the door. It seemed as though he was getting a baby out of the car. As I watched, I wondered if the person I was looking at was that asshole, Jeff Kathrein, who had robbed me and the others.

He seemed to be having a problem with getting the baby out of the car. Only it wasn't a baby! It was a kid who appeared to be completely out of it, as if he had been doped up.

I started thinking the kid was in trouble and that this guy was abducting him or something, so I didn't take my eyes off of them. The kid appeared to be a young teenager, and the man I suspected as the robber (and possible kidnapper) grabbed the kid's hand and guided him toward the spa, almost as though the kid were blind. *This is really weird,* I thought to myself. Even more odd was how the kid was walking on his tiptoes half the time.

At this point I had completely forgotten about Travolta, and I was sure I was witnessing an abduction. I got out of my car and followed them, but when I got inside the spa, I didn't see them. Out of the corner of my eye, I caught a glimpse of them going into the restroom. I followed in close behind them. There they were, with the guy unzipping the kid's pants to pee.

"Is everything okay?" I asked.

"Mind your own business. My son needs to pee."

I backed off, but I knew it was not his son, because right then, it hit me. This was John Travolta's son, Jett, and I noticed the guy was wearing Travolta's wedding ring. It further dawned on me, that was why Travolta was without it earlier!

I couldn't fathom it. John Travolta had stooped to a whole new low. He was now bringing his son along when he looked for dick, and leaving the poor boy in the car for hours, like a dog. Moreover, at this point, I realized the boy's handler was Jeff Kathrein, the guy boarding the plane who Travolta was kissing in the famous "Travolta Kisses Strange Men" picture.

I was appalled at how poorly Jett was treated. He was a really big boy who had obviously been doped up. I followed Jeff Kathrein and Jett. Jett kept trying to go inside the spa, as though he wanted to find his dad. *How sad is this?* I was thinking, but Kathrein kept pulling him outside to the car. They got back in the Dakota, and I could see Kathrein force-feeding Jett some sort of pill. Jett reluctantly took it.

About thirty minutes went by, and finally, John Travolta exited the spa. I had the perfect view for when Travolta got into the Dakota. He sat in the back, next to Jett. Poor Jett, he had to wait in the car while his father was busy cruising for sex. As Travolta, Kathrein, and Jett drive away, I started taking pictures of their departure.

I couldn't help but think that Travolta was a scumbag, and a pervert, who put his dick before his child! I was ashamed of John Travolta now more than ever. I was sure Kelly didn't have a clue what her husband did at the spa, and especially no clue what he had been doing with their child in tow. It was a very sad thing, what I witnessed that day…

Very sad.

I hoped poor Jett Travolta got the attention and the help he most definitely needed. Only time would tell.

Chapter 29

LIONS SPA

This was to be the last spa I would join in my efforts to try to get away from Travolta. For a moment in time, it was my little hidden, nonperverted spa, and I loved it! The owners, in comparison to Century Spa and its owners, are truly sweet people. If I could, I would probably omit them from this book, but I can't. This is a true story, not fiction, so I'm writing it exactly as it went down.

Lions Spa is the spa that Kurt Russell got caught coming out of years ago by the tabloids. It is a place where you can get your massage and your rocks off. I, of course, indulged in both. My masseuse's name was Sarah. She happened to be in room six that day, and boy did she make that room rock!

For the most part, Lions Spa is a straight spa where men go and get a massage. For twenty dollars more, a hand job. At least that's what I got. Imagine my disbelief when I saw John Travolta there. This spa had very few gays going there, so what was John doing there?

This was different turf for him, and he was cruising it just like the other spas. Initially I thought, *How sad.* He had stooped to a whole new low in his predatory search for cock. He was a big-time movie star, and this was a small, quaint little spa. But there he was.

This, most definitely, would be the last spa I ever joined.

There were only a few times I would ever see, speak to, or spy on John Travolta in person again. I had made up my mind. There was no way of getting away from John Travolta, other than to heed the words of the title to my book, *You'll Never Spa in This Town Again*, and I decided once and for all to never spa in a public facility again.

I'm hoping that *You'll Never Spa in This Town Again* will apply to John Travolta as well, or at the very least, he'll be aware that more people will do as I've done—tell their story.

Chapter 30

TRAVOLTA DREAM
June 2, 2008

I had the craziest dream last night. I dreamt I ran into John Travolta at a spa. In my dream, I didn't recognize the spa, and the minute I saw Travolta, I anticipated telling him about my book, but I couldn't reach him. Every time I tried to approach him to tell him, he disappeared into a steam room with some guy. At least, even in my dreams, Travolta's consistent!

I eventually chased him down and told him, "If you don't stop all this lewd behavior in public, I'm going through with my book."

"Who cares? No one will believe you," he replied with an almost evil laugh.

Then all the guys in the spa started to chase me. Naturally, I wanted to run, but I couldn't move my legs. The whole time Travolta was laughing at me and telling the guys to throw me out of his house. His house? Now I was at his home and trying to escape the guys chasing me.

The last thing I remember in the dream is Travolta flying over his house in an airplane, and I was tied up in his garage. Like a villain fleeing the scene. *Wow! What a weird dream that was!*

When I woke up, I thought about the dream and what it meant. They say your dreams have meaning. I wondered if it was because I felt bad about my book and what it might do to Travolta, or was it just a stupid dream about a stupid man I'd written a book about?

I don't know. I had never had a dream about Travolta in all the years I had been watching him. *How odd for me to have one now,* I thought.

Chapter 31

TRAVOLTA ENCOUNTER
June 8, 2008

I went to Lions Spa on June 8, 2008 and ran into an old friend from City Spa I hadn't seen in years. Almost instantly we were catching up on old times at City Spa.

With a "you'll never guess" tone, he asked me, "Guess who I ran into here at the Lions Spa last week?"

"I don't know, who?"

"Our friend from City Spa, John Travolta. He was so out of control when I saw him. He even asked me, 'Hey, where are all the Mexican guys?'" he said, laughing. "I looked at him and said, 'In Mexico.' Travolta fired back, 'I'm going to Santa Fe, New Mexico, and I'll get some Mexican meat while I'm down there.' I was so surprised to find Travolta, in a little Korean spa, asking where the Mexican guys were."

Apparently, Travolta was cruising Korean dick, but craving Mexican meat. That shows he's out of his mind. That's like going to Sushi King and asking for a burrito!

"I've never seen Travolta so bold. He kept disappearing into the back room with guys, one right after the other, like the Harry Houdini of cocks. Travolta displayed a total lack of concern with regards to who knew he was gay. While I was at the spa, Travolta was hitting on everyone who came in, and in a horny stupor even hit on a straight guy who told him to fuck off, that he wasn't gay."

My friend had tons of firsthand accounts of Travolta. Once he started, the information just kept flowing.

"I thought that might have stopped Travolta, but no luck. He continued on for several hours that day. I was there for three hours. When I left, Travolta was still going strong."

We talked about how sad Travolta's actions were and, at the same time, how gross it was. We both knew it would only be a matter of time before he got caught in the act. During our conversation, I never mentioned the book I had written. He felt as I did, that it was time for Travolta to get some help for his addiction, and that if he didn't find some way to control his urge to continue risky behavior at spas, it would only be a matter of time until he would be forced out of the closet as opposed to coming out on his own. Imagine getting arrested for sexual misconduct at a public facility!

It seems everyone who has known of Travolta's cock-cruising ways agrees he's worse with every passing day, taking more and more chances with his behavior. What a shame! What a sorrowful story. But he's a sexual pervert, and he deserves to be stopped from masturbating in front of people. I, for one, am sick of his lewd, disgusting, and filthy behavior.

He's gone too far for too long, and when he took poor Jett to the spa with him in 2007, that was the end of me feeling sorry for Mr. Travolta. He's a self-centered, sexually deviated, closeted homosexual, and I can't wait for the rest of the world to know the real Travolta.

Chapter 32

TRAVOLTA
FINAL ENCOUNTER
October 19, 2008

If ever in my life did I need a steam, it was this night. My best friend in the world, Lorrie, had had a terrible accident. She fell down a flight of stairs and broke her neck. She remained on life support until October 5, 2008, when she passed away. If that wasn't bad enough, my mother unexpectedly passed away on October 17, 2008.

I hadn't had a steam in weeks, and I needed one badly, to clear my head and just cry. The loss of my best friend and my wonderful mother was so devastating to me, and affected me so heavily, that I was in a fog, and I knew the only thing that could possibly help me would be a steam.

It was around eight in the evening of October 19, 2008, when I headed for the Lions Spa for a steam. I knew I'd have to hurry because they closed early, at nine o'clock, and I'd barely have an hour. I could have used several hours that night. If you've never steamed and felt the benefits to your body, you should. It can do wonders for your mind, body, and soul.

As I parked my car and headed into the spa, John Travolta was the furthest thing from my mind. I had shelved all those silly dreams of him and I years go, and had actually gone out of my way over the years to avoid him at all costs.

I could feel my mind already starting to clear as I approached the entrance. Just the thought of steaming alone was helpful at this point. Little did I know, within a few seconds, I'd be standing face-to-face with John Travolta. Again. And again, as usual, he would be looking for sex. As soon as I made my way into the locker room, there was Travolta looking as terrible as ever.

His head was shaved, and his face was adorned with a thick, heavy mustache. He looked like shit. He was fat, too. He didn't even try to suck it in. Travolta had put on so much weight that the towel had no chance of wrapping around him (not that he ever wore one). Travolta had been reduced to one big fabulous celebrity mess!

The first thing I thought was, *Oh my God, not tonight, I need my steam.* But, as usual, it was John in rare form, with his erect penis making its debut as soon as he saw me walk through the locker room door. I was sick to my stomach at the sight of the pervert, and I wanted nothing to do with him.

As soon as our eyes met, he said, "Hello, Rob, long time no see."

"Yeah, long time," I replied noncommittally.

I didn't know what to say or do. I was stuck. I had already finished my manuscript for *You'll Never Spa in This Town Again*, and now here he was, writing himself another chapter on his antics. Just when I thought there was no more to write about John Travolta, he showed up in front of me with his penis in hand.

I made my way past him to the shower, praying he would leave me alone, and thank God he did, for a minute anyway. I don't know where he wandered off to, but I was glad I could have a minute to myself.

Just as I finished showering, Travolta came waltzing by, shaking his penis. It was all very revolting to me at this stage in the game. I made it clear with the look I gave him to stay away from me. He went straight into the steam room and stood there, waiting for me to come in. He's so ballsy and doesn't take no for no. There was no way in hell I was going in there.

I didn't care if it would make for another filthy chapter on him or not; I was getting out of there. I decided to go around a corner and see if he left, but no, I watched him stand there in the steam room at full arousal and masturbate while he waited for someone else to come in.

That was it, the last straw!

I made my way to the locker room and quickly dressed to get out of there, but not fast enough. I was leaving when Travolta walked in and said, "What's wrong with you tonight?"

I looked right at him. "You! You're what's wrong with me tonight, and I'm leaving!"

If eyes could talk, his would have said, *"Fuck you."* I didn't care. I was gone. I didn't stick around in the parking lot as I'd done so many times back in the day when I was pursuing him. I didn't care to see him leave, I didn't care to ever see him again, and the only way to make sure that happened was to never spa in this or any other town again! I couldn't help but reflect on the long journey I had had with John Travolta, and all the time, energy, and money I had invested in it. I knew this was the end tonight.

Though my days as a regular at City Spa are behind me, I still pop in every now and then. I spent the last several years dodging John Travolta for the most part, but there were those times when he'd show up and I would document it for the book. It seemed no matter what I did, every spa I went to…there he was! Although it did appear he had moved on from City Spa as well. I lost what little bit of respect I had left for Travolta years ago, and he was now just an obstacle I had to avoid on a regular basis if I wanted to go to a steam room.

Chapter 33

JETT TRAVOLTA
1/4/2009

I couldn't believe the news I was hearing. Jett Travolta had passed away at sixteen years of age.

I had just gotten settled in my new home, and I was eagerly awaiting January 15 to arrive. That was the date I had chosen to do the press release. I was excited to finally be doing it, no matter what the outcome.

I was preparing myself for the worst. I'd already received death threats. At that point, I felt it best to sell the home I had been living in and get something else to live in where nobody could find me. I had accomplished that and was settled in my place in time for Christmas. It seemed too good to be true. All I had to do was chill until the fifteenth and see what happened—so I thought.

Knowing Jett had passed away, there was no way I could go through with the press release as planned. In fact, it would have to be put on hold.

I was advised by my attorney, and even friends, to go through with my original press release date on the fifteenth anyway. Their reasoning was that I could ride the coattails of the media exposure following Jett's death, but there was no way I could go through with it knowing how difficult this ordeal had to be on John and Kelly.

I didn't want to add any pain to their situation at all. I can't imagine what the loss of a child is like on a parent, but I'm sure it's unbearable. No matter what I thought of John Travolta and his dirty steam bath hookups, I was not going to add to his grief.

So I decided to put it on hold for a year and let them heal. I would have never thought in a million years that during that time they would already replace poor Jett with a new baby. *Wow!* How sad for poor Jett to be thought of as something that could be replaced so quickly. Why didn't they adopt? That would have been better. If they were in so much pain that they felt the need to have another child so quickly, why couldn't they have adopted?

Before Jett Travolta passed away, when I wrote about that day at Century Spa when John was there with his son in 2007, I edited it down because I was thinking of Jett. I tried to clean up that chapter in case he got wind of it. Once Jett passed away, I knew I could put the original chapter back in, with all its graphic details of a sex addict on a mission with his son in tow.

Out of respect for the family, I feel I have done my part in holding back from releasing my book. With their broken family so magically fixed, as only Hollywood can do, it is all fair game now.

Chapter 34

THE MASSEURS REVISITED
2009

Milena

Joseph

Vladimir

Serge

MILENA

2009

I ran into Milena in 2009, at the Grove, as she was on her way to give a massage to a client. We exchanged numbers, but I think we both knew right then and there we wouldn't be calling one another. Now, I would like to hear from her. I hope she likes *You'll Never Spa in This Town Again*. It wouldn't have been the same without her.

JOSEPH

2009

Joseph is no longer working at City Spa. I'm sorry to say he is on dialysis and in very poor health. Needless to say, there will be no 2009 update on Travolta from him. Joseph is truly a very sweet man whom I care for. I'm sorry if my book hurts him in any way, as that was never my intention. Joseph and I were friends at City Spa for many years and even wrote a song together. He's an amazing person and composer. I wish him the best.

VLADIMIR

2009

It's January 8, 2009. John Travolta's son, Jett Travolta, passed away just five days earlier, and I wanted to go back to City Spa and do one last interview/massage with Vladimir.

I had always planned on doing one last interview with all the masseurs in 2008, then release my book in January of 2009, but my plans took many different directions that affected the timeline I had in mind. With Jett's untimely passing, I didn't know how to bring up Travolta. Luckily, I didn't have to, because Vladimir did.

He started by saying how sorry he was for John and his loss. I could smell booze on his breath as he gave me my massage. Then he just blurted out, "Rob, something is very fishy with Jett's passing. You know, the nanny is also John's boyfriend."

"Really?" I responded.

"Oh yeah, he has been for quite some time now."

I just lay there and listened.

"That poor little boy," he continued.

"What do you mean by that?"

"John always acted like he was embarrassed of his son. I once asked John if it were true that Jett was autistic, and he was quick to say his son was absolutely not autistic. He said his son was in school in Switzerland and would soon be following in his footsteps to becoming an actor."

Vladimir said he knew back then that John was lying, and now, in 2009, the real truth was coming out.

Vladimir said, while Jett was laying there dying after his fall in the bathroom, the reason so many hours went by before anyone discovered Jett was due to the fact that Travolta and Katherine were in John's bedroom having sex. Poor Jett just laid there and died due to his father's lack of concern for his son. Apparently, Katherine was too busy fucking daddy Travolta to tend to poor little Jett.

The last thing Vladimir said to me was, "I can only hope John regrets how he treated his son now."

SERGE
2009

The date was 1/23/09. I went back to City Spa and got a scrub from Serge and casually asked, "Have you seen Travolta?"

"That pervert doesn't come here anymore, because he's concerned someone will take his picture. I don't know why he cares. John Travolta is gay. Everyone here at City Spa knows that. One time, when I gave Travolta a massage upstairs in the private room, Travolta specifically asked me to rub his asshole. Not just the butt cheeks, but the hole. He wanted it rubbed and massaged. Travolta has asked every one of the masseurs the same thing. Word gets around. Some of them obliged him; some didn't. I finally had to tell him, 'I'm not a proctologist, and I'm not rubbing your anus.'"

Travolta told him he would tip him very well. Serge seemed upset, as if he was venting and glad to get it off his chest.

"I was disgusted, and that after that, I never gave Travolta another private massage. I would only do body scrubs downstairs, where other people were present.

Thankfully, John never asked me again. Travolta is a pervert. I've watched him walk around City Spa for years playing with his dick and gawking at all the guys."

I told Serge that I had seen Travolta at Century Spa and what I had witnessed. More venting ensued.

"John Travolta is a homosexual and a liar. I can't stand him. It doesn't surprise me that Travolta would bring his son along while he cruises for dick. I can't wait until the day comes when that bastard gets caught."

I wanted to tell Serge all about my book, but I knew better. In time, he'd know.

A few minutes passed by, and he started up again.

"Jett Travolta is in a better place now. I've always felt sorry for Jett, because John was ashamed of him. Whenever I would ask him about his kids, John would only speak of his daughter. He never once spoke of his son. Apparently his embarrassment of his son runs deep."

How sad.

Chapter 35

THE CELEBRITIES

John Amos

Jeff Conaway

John Cusack

Andy Dick

Paul Giamatti

George Michael

Mystery Microphallus Movie Star

Jeremy Piven

Kurt Russel

Pauly Shore

Jean Claude Van Damme

Billy Zane

John Travolta

JOHN AMOS
Packin' (MD)

John Amos is definitely straight, and a really nice man. Even better is the fact that he's not homophobic at all. I first met him through Milena, during the "Revamping of Rob" for the Travolta period. Milena had recently played matchmaker between John Amos and one of her girlfriends, and we would all go out for drinks together from time to time. The things Milena's girlfriend would tell us about Amos's sexual habits would shock us. She told us that she couldn't stand him. It was apparent that she was using him for something, but for what wasn't really made clear to me. I would run into Amos quite frequently at City Spa, and we would have dinner together. I really wanted to tell him he was being played by Milena's friend, but decided to stay out of it. I recall thinking it was really sad, this relationship that he was in, because he spoke so highly of Milena when all she was doing was setting him up.

Milena invited me to dinner by the dock in Marina del Rey, where John's boat was. By the time we got there, John was drunk and really out of it. John's girlfriend, whose name I still can't remember for the life of me, put John to bed and then started to trash him in front of us. The saddest part of this trashing was she told us she had another boyfriend on the side and how she was madly in love with him. She said a lot of things that were trashy about John Amos, and the next time I saw him at City Spa, my heart broke for him. The other thing was this girl, the con, on top of all these things, was racist. She kept referring to John as "the nigger." Shortly after our dinner on the boat, I heard that the con dumped John and married her true love. John definitely deserved better than that.

For the first time, I saw a completely different side of my dear Milena. With her, everything had its price. Not only did I tip Milena well, but once I landed Travolta, she expected I would get Travolta to finally let her massage him so he would see how good she was and would ask for her massage services in the future. This wasn't too nasty of a deal for me, but backstabbing her client, John Amos, a lonely middle-aged man and introducing him to a con woman was, definitely a raw deal. Milena wanted what she wanted, and she would do anything to get it.

John Amos was on a hit show again, called *Men in Trees*, and, in my opinion, he deserved it. I wish him the best. In the last few years, every time I would run into him at City Spa, he'd ask me if I had seen Milena and if I had her number because he had lost it. He told me that he needed one of Milena's massages, but couldn't locate her. I bet after reading this, he will never want a massage from her again.

Because John Amos has always been a gentleman around me, I will not go into further details about the other things the con woman mentioned. After all, who knows if she was even telling the truth about those tales of the bedroom, but if she were, he's as kinky as they come!

JEFF CONAWAY
Unknown

I was browsing through one of the Hollywood trade magazines' classified ads section and came across this ad from Jeff Conaway stating he was teaching acting classes. I knew he had been in *Grease* with John Travolta, and was also Travolta's roommate years earlier. Everyone knew him from the character he portrayed on the TV show *Taxi*. However, that was a while back, and now everyone in Hollywood knew he was a messed-up drug addict. Even so, I couldn't resist calling him regarding the ad he had posted.

I was shocked when Jeff himself answered the phone. He was hammered. A complete mess. But he could still conduct business, or so I guessed. On and on he babbled about what he could offer me as my acting coach before making it a point to let me know all he had done to help make John Travolta a star. He kept my ears hostage as he told me, at length, how John was an inconsiderate bastard and had never ever done shit for him. He was acting like a tweaker telling their sorry-ass sob story.

I knew I had hit the jackpot with Jeff. He had been reduced to an out-of-work has-been, actor and current drug addict. I just knew he would be a great source of information about Travolta, and all I'd have to do is take a few acting lessons and listen to him ramble.

Interestingly, it was Halloween when I called Jeff, and by the time we were done talking, he was acting like he had known me all my life.

"Rob, it's Halloween. Me and my lady are going to some parties tonight. Why don't you come and go with us?"

At first, I was hesitant, because as fucked up as he sounded on the phone, I could only imagine what he'd be like in person. However, I also knew this was an opportunity that I couldn't pass up. So I jotted down his home address, which was somewhere up in the foothills of Hollywood.

A few more minutes of conversation, and I said, "Great, I'll be there at eight!"

"No, come now," he said, "and bring some alcohol."

I remember thinking, *It's five o'clock in the afternoon.*

I decided to go for this roller-coaster ride with Jeff Conaway and his lady, so I headed out. I could have never been prepared for what I witnessed when I got there. Jeff was fucked up, and he and his lady friend were now fighting like cats and dogs.

The first thing he said when he met me was, "You look like a little like Travolta. Did you bring booze?"

"I sure did."

Instead of going to any parties, we hung out at his house. All night long he talked about "Travolta the Horrible."

"You know, Rob, all those rumors about John being gay are true. Back in the day, John would always put the moves on me. We eventually hooked up on several occasions." According to Jeff, as I had been told before, John was a bottom.

Jeff went on to tell me that back in the day, when he and Travolta were just starting their acting careers, they were best of friends. And though he was straight and John was gay, they were very similar in many ways. Jeff said there were many occasions when they would have sex after partying, doing drugs, and drinking. Travolta would always seduce him, starting with a blow job and finishing with full-blown anal with John as the bottom. Even though Jeff claimed John's ass was as loose as a goose, he still bragged about how many times he'd fucked that loose hole of Travolta's.

You could see all the abuse Jeff's body had gone through due to the alcohol and drugs. I never saw him do any drugs in front of me, but he would leave the room every thirty or forty minutes, and ten minutes later he'd walk back into the room perky as can be.

I knew one night, this Halloween night, with Jeff Conaway was all I would need. He told me more about his and Travolta's antics than I could have hoped for. Although I led him to believe I would be back for acting lessons, I knew there would be no need to see him again.

He kept declaring, "I can make you a star if you listen to me." Then, out of nowhere, he rejuvenated my interest with, "If you want to meet Travolta, I can arrange it."

I didn't act interested in Travolta and played it cool. It was truly sad to see Jeff Conaway the way I saw him that night. I felt very sorry for him. He was still holding on to a drug addict's dream of being on top again. He was the classic case of an addict in complete denial of his drug problem.

Oddly, he kept saying, "I don't even drink, but since it's Halloween, why not?"

Yeah, right, I thought, *like Halloween is a celebratory cause for inebriation.*

It took me hours to jockey for position toward his front door. He continued to ramble on as if I were the last person on the planet. Good Lord, I was more than ready to leave. I'd heard all I cared to hear, and I'd seen way too much of this broken man. Jeff Conaway, at some point, was a star. How sad to see what drugs will do to and take from a person. I finally made it out of there before the sun came up. We had been drinking all night, and he cried his heart out. When I look back on it now, it was fun, but at the time, it didn't feel that way at all.

I was only after Travolta information, not every other aspect of Jeff Conaway's life. As I left, I wished him the best. I remember thinking, *It won't be long before he departs the planet.*

Soon thereafter, he had cleaned up his act and was certainly singing a different tune about Travolta in the media. It was suddenly John Travolta, the wonderful friend. Hmm! I hope it was all true. I hope John did help out poor little Jeff Conaway, because he certainly needed it.

JOHN CUSACK
Packin' (LG)

John and I have sat side by side in the steam rooms at City Spa for years. Unlike a lot of celebrities, he is very good-looking in person, and he is not only approachable, but also gifted in his manhood. Unfortunately for the gay community, I've never once seen anything from him that would lead me to believe that he is gay.

Many of the City Spa staff said he was and that they had caught him in the heat of the moment many times, but I never did. But there was this guy who was a regular at City Spa who claimed to be Cusack's architect. He would try to impress guys by telling them he was Cusack's architect and close friend. He would go on about how he'd remodeled John's home in Chicago. While at these homes, he said he partook in many parties that Cusack would host with his entourage. We've all heard the phrase "anything goes." Well, these parties were the epitome of that, so he claimed. I continued listening to this guy talking about Cusack having a sweet tooth for orgies filled with well-hung men. According to him, Cusack would get very kinky with his sex, including, but not limited to, *golden showers* and *scat*. Most definitely all the boys got very dirty playing, and when the fun was done, everyone would take a much-needed shower together.

As I said before, I myself never saw any behavior from John Cusack indicating he was gay, but there were always stories floating around that would lead me to question his sexual preference. However, he appeared to be using the spa for its intended purposes whenever I would see him.

ANDY DICK
Lackin' (SM)

What can I say about Andy Dick that hasn't been said? He's truly weird. I've never seen him at City Spa, only at Century Spa. He would always come with an entourage of young boys who followed him around as though he was really something. Who knows? Maybe, to them, he was.

Andy's group loved to sit far back in the steam room and stare out at all the naked men. Those guys could stay in the steam room forever. They never seemed to get overheated. The boys he had with him were gorgeous, especially the one who appeared to be his boyfriend. Andy would always be telling him what to do and how to groom himself to his liking, everything from how to shave to how to wear his hair.

Andy's truly at a loss for attractiveness, and I feel bad for saying it. He was always staring. He would eye me and then go out of his way to watch me shower and then give me a big smile afterward. He treated me like a man whose dick he wanted to suck. I always turned down his advances toward me.

One time, while Andy was getting his dick sucked by his boyfriend in the steam room, I walked in. Luckily for me, they got up and walked out. They went to another room to finish fucking, with four guys in tow. The straight guys complained to the owner that Andy and his group were getting it on in front of everyone, but that was just Andy. He was always such a raunchy diva. It was customary for Andy to be donning a towel on his head like a turban and ordering his entourage around. "Go get me some water" and "Get me a razor" were among a barrage of demanding commands that would come out of Andy's mouth, always followed by "Go, go, go!" Andy was different with me, though. He didn't treat me like a member of his entourage.

They were always up to something dirty and nasty. They most certainly went back and forth to the Rock Room, where most of the sucking and fucking went on. It was the popular hot spot if sex was on your mind, and everybody knew about it.

When it was time to leave the spa, Andy would clap his hands twice, like "chop-chop," and before you knew it, they would be all packed up and gone. The guy I think was his boyfriend would always chauffeur Andy to the spa. I say "chauffeur" because Andy was always sitting in the passenger's seat whenever I would see them coming or leaving the parking lot. But I seem to remember Andy got into a lot of vehicular trouble back then, having accidents and then running from the scene, so he must have been either following court orders not to drive or he was just being a diva. Again, who knows?

PAUL GIAMATTI
Packin' (XLG)

I only saw him there once, but I will never forget all that I saw. Long before running into Mr. Giamatti near the showers, his reputation had been the topic of many a steam room conversation amongst the gays.

You'd hear it from different people at different times: "I lust for Giamatti's dick" and "Paul Giamatti has the biggest cock."

I asked some of my fellow steamers was it true about Giamatti's dick, and they all replied with a flat-out and resounding yes. But then there would be the audible sigh as they continued, "Baby, it's huge, but he's straight."

Apparently, plenty of them had tried many times to get with that cock of his. It was common knowledge at all the spas, well, in the gay circle, that Paul Giamatti was packin' big-time.

Now this is a guy, after looking at his dick, you'd think absolutely slept his way to the top. If it wasn't for his obvious overabundance of acting skills, I'd bet anything his dick was what opened the doors in Hollywood for him. Literally! I never heard a bad thing about Giamatti from any of the masseurs or employees. No one. And, in that circle, that was very rare. I never saw him there again, but I would hear things about when he had been there. Pretty much always the same thing—all the gays in the place buzzin' about Giamatti's manhood.

GEORGE MICHAEL
Packin' (LG)

One of my experiences at City Spa was witnessing what I call "The Downfall of George Michael," and it would be through my encounters with his boyfriend, Kenny Goss, that would make it all possible. The first time I ever saw Kenny was when he was pulling into the parking lot of City Spa in a flashy yellow Hummer. He had just arrived in Los Angeles from Texas. He moved to Hollywood with the intentions of hooking up with a gay celebrity, partying around the clock, and just enjoying his life in style…so he said. There was no denying that Kenny, at the time, had all the looks and undeniable sex appeal a man could possess, but even so, it was more than obvious the clock was not ticking in his favor.

According to Kenny, "I have no time to waste finding and hooking up with a celebrity."

He wanted to "hook it up" right then and there, and it seemed like no one would be able to stop him. Kenny was blond, of average height, and had a beautiful ass! The nicest bubble butt from Texas you could ever imagine. Angus beef, anyone? The moment Kenny came sashaying through the door with his towel around his waist, I noticed his perfect sun-kissed tan and his ruggedly handsome face. Oh, and to top it off, he had a hint of naughty boy in him.

After a short time of knowing Kenny, he spoke of this famous celebrity he was dating, and for a while, I was afraid it was Travolta. He talked about the drugs they indulged in and how they would have threesomes all the time. After a few conversations with him, including the description of his secret celebrity lover, I was sure it wasn't Travolta.

A while passed; then one day Kenny introduced me to his secret celebrity lover at City Spa. It was none other than George Michael! Kenny landed George Michael only a month after he moved to Los Angeles. George's face looked strange, somewhat in a daze, and downright scary. I came to realize later that he was high and Kenny liked him that way because he could boss him around.

Their relationship began, unsurprisingly, with a lot of partying and drug use. Kenny was a bad influence on George Michael. And when I say bad, I mean b-a-d, bad!

According to Kenny, they both liked to use street drugs like heroin, ecstasy, cocaine, crystal meth, and K, which are drugs that apparently free your sexual inhibitions. (FYI, K is ketamine, similar to PCP.) After seeing those two high, I didn't want to have anything to do with them. Kenny was obsessed with sex. He followed me around at the spa like a sick pervert, making frequent attempts to drop his towel in order to try to grab my attention. I didn't give him so much as the time of day, but it didn't stop him from continuously dropping his towel in front of me every time he'd see me. Kenny also had this habit of stroking his cock in front of me or anyone else around him. Personally, I found it disgusting.

Kenny changed drastically after landing George Michael. He believed, somehow, after landing him, that he was now a man of importance. He was overly aggressive, and he wouldn't take no for an answer. If you knew Kenny Goss like I knew Kenny Goss, it would have come as no surprise that George Michael got busted in a public Beverly Hills bathroom attempting to give a blow job to a cop. In fact, Kenny was the culprit who had taught him the art of "sexual cruising." It was these lessons that led to the famous bathroom arrest, and ultimately forced the "coming out" of George Michael.

No, it is not true that George Michael was set up, as he announced on national television. Oh please, George! By then he was a full-blown whore. He definitely was not a father figure by any stretch of the imagination. (Pun intended.) George, like his boyfriend Kenny, would frequently expose himself at the spa, and he had no problem jacking off in front of complete strangers. It seemed that George really enjoyed shocking people. He was off the deep end, to say the least.

In time, George Michael started to get caught sucking dick at truck stops, public parks, and other random places. He would try to defend himself by explaining he was a normal gay man doing what normal gay guys do. In no way is

George Michael a gay spokesperson or an advocate. He is a disgrace to the gay population because he degrades himself and then makes up bogus excuses of why he was in the bushes, the truck stop, and all the places where he was caught doing his thing. George is the poster child for lewd sexual misconduct in public places. It didn't take me long to realize what a loser Kenny Goss was and how he led George Michael down a path of sexual perversity and pure destruction. Kenny Goss, more like Kenny Gross!

When George Michael lost his mother and was heartbroken, Kenny was there for him and ready to kill his pain with drugs and more lewd sexual behavior. Michael went through his mourning in despair and alone. Kenny Gross, I mean, Goss, was too busy thinking of the dirty games he could play with others while cruising for his next sexual victim.

I can assure you, if George Michael's mother knew how he was behaving, she would have rolled over in her grave. I pitied him, and I thought of offering my advice, *See the light with that user loser and move on.* Being that I am not one for conflict, I decided, again, to keep my advice and opinion to myself.

One day, I saw George Michael at the spa by himself, and I slid a note into his locker. Kenny somehow got ahold of this note. He called and told me to leave George Michael, his boyfriend, alone and that he would kill me if I didn't back off. He was high as a kite. Kenny knew exactly how to manipulate George Michael. Talk about being at the right place at the right time: George Michael was going through a vulnerable time in his life. He had been out of the limelight for a while, then his mother passed away, and Kenny was there to take full advantage.

In the beginning, Kenny was an interesting enough person to listen to. As time went on, and after hearing countless accounts of excessive drugs and sex, I didn't want to hear another lousy word from him. It got to the point where I would go out of my way to avoid him when I'd see him coming toward me. I was fed up with this Kenny Goss character and was sick of him hitting on me. This went on for years at City Spa. Kenny would hit on guys in a premeditated plot to reel in the bait for him and George Michael. Finally, one day, I bluntly told Kenny to back off and that a threesome with him and George Michael was not going to happen.

It appeared that George was an excellent student of the Kenny Goss school of fast living. One Saturday evening, I went to City Spa, and the place was packed with gays cruising for straight cock. George Michael was right there in the thick of it. On this particular night, he was cruising for sex without Kenny anywhere in sight. When I wandered into the dry sauna, I was surprised to see two old men having sex with George. While he was getting fucked, he sucked the other old dude's dick. It was not a pretty sight, to say the least. And they didn't let me seeing them stop them. In fact, by the time they finished their orgy of filth, there were at least seven guys in there watching, and masturbating as well. Shocking to see? Yes. But it really was just a typical night at the spa.

Kenny Goss's appearance changed over the years I knew him. He would no longer grab your attention because of his stunning appearance. Kenny looked like a typical druggie whom the spirit of life had left a long time ago. His bubble butt was now flat, and his face-lift made him look like a drag queen. Saying Kenny looked used up is an understatement.

I'm glad to hear that George Michael realized how Kenny Goss tainted him all those years and got rid of that filth. When it comes to Kenny, I'm being very kind, because I could go into detail a lot deeper.

Kenny and George were like fixtures at City Spa for a few years. I'll never forget this one day, when I had just gotten a wonderful massage from Vladimir and was getting ready to leave, when I passed through the dark TV room and, to my surprise, there was George Michael sitting alone in the corner. As I approached closer to where he was sitting, I could see a needle protruding from his arm and a few droplets of blood. I don't know what was in it, but whatever it was it had George Michael high as a kite.

I felt sorrow for him because he was a complete mess. I talked to him for a few moments, said good-bye, and walked away. He followed me until I got dressed and left. It was very sad to see how lost he was. Only time will tell if George Michael gets himself back together. I certainly hope he does. It could only be a matter of time before he'll get busted again or maybe even found dead. I certainly hope not.

MYSTERY MICROPHALLUS
MOVIE STAR
Lackin' (Poor Guy)

I met the MMMS soon after joining City Spa. His body of work is up there with the best actors of all time. Unfortunately for the MMMS, his physical body is a far cry different. In fact, "microphallus" is the medical term used to describe a medical condition that is just about the worst thing that could happen to a man. By definition, microphallus is a congenital underdevelopment of the penis.

I had heard about the famous movie star and his horrible affliction soon after joining the spa. On several occasions, some of the regular gays who were there would talk about him while in the steam room, things like "Can you believe how little his dick is?" and "If my dick was that little, I'd cut it off and get in line for gender reassignment." They would say the most terrible jokes.

One day, while I was in the shower, in walked the MMMS. I could not believe how good-looking he was in person. I couldn't stop looking at his gorgeous face, and when I did, I was in absolute shock! None, not even one, of those cruel jokes about his manhood could have prepared me for what I saw. Or better yet, what I didn't see. This beautiful movie star, a hunk, no less, standing there in all his glory. Just like in the movies, it seemed as though everything was moving in slow motion. His teeth sparkled as he smiled, and then you looked down between his legs and he was missing his dick. Was he a movie star, or had Ken left Barbie at home to enjoy a day at the spa?

I just stood there...staring, when he wasn't looking. Oh my God! What a tragedy! This certainly showed he made it in Hollywood on pure talent. There's no way he could have ever slept his way to the top. Ever. I introduced myself when the time was right and told him I was a big fan, which is something I don't normally tell an actor even if it is true, but in this case, I felt I had just met a victim of a horrific, life-changing tragedy, and I felt so sorry for his terrible loss.

I have no doubt that he is straight. I have never seen him looking at a guy or behaving in a sexual way. I wonder. If a man has zero in the dick department, does he even have a sex drive? You could tell when he talked about his kids how happy he was with his life. Wait. Kids? Well, I guess it doesn't curb your sexual appetite at all. Then again, he could adopt, and there's the surrogate option. Guess I'll have to keep on wondering. Either way, you could tell he was happy with his life.

There was a time when he had a hit show on TV and a hit in the movie theaters at the same time. He is one of America's favorite actors, who has given us so much and who has never shown any sign of lewd behavior at the spa in any way, shape, or form. For those reasons, I'm withholding his name—the only name on my journey that I'm not going to tell. And why should I? He is so decent and moral that he tries to keep his towel around him at all times. Either it's due to good morality or the embarrassment of what it would reveal. Sometimes the towel slips and he's so embarrassed in front of whoever might have seen his tragic secret—another reason why this is one secret I'm not telling. I can't imagine what it would be like to be one of the world's biggest stars and to be thought of as a sex symbol, when all along you know for a fact you have no penis. It must be difficult at best to live with, and I for one, refuse to add to that.

JEREMY PIVEN
Packin' (XLG)

The only thing bigger than Jeremy Piven's ego…is his dick!

I met Jeremy at City Spa during his *Ellen* days. He was real friendly to everyone back then, but as his career grew, so did his ego. Before long, he became closed off to most everyone around him. I never saw Jeremy up to anything but steaming—steaming for the right reasons. He was most definitely a regular at the spa. He lived for his steam. Erin, the masseuse, gave massages to Jeremy for years.

Erin said that Jeremy was obsessed with his hair loss and repeatedly asked Erin what he thought he should do about it. He also told me Jeremy had been to Bosley for a hair transplant consultation and would have the procedure done when he got enough time off from work. I've always heard that short men can be packing big sticks, but I never believed it until I met Jeremy Piven. The man is hung like a horse. Whenever he would walk around the spa, all the guys would stare at his dick. Even the straight ones! It just jumps out at you. And you can tell, he is definitely used to the attention that comes with being so overly endowed. To top it off, his naked body is beautifully sculpted and tan. One look at him, and you can see this is a man who takes care of himself. His body is definitely a testament to that!

But, like I said earlier, as his career grew, so did his ego. Only it wasn't proportionate, because he started acting so unapproachable, as if her were now some Shakespearean actor. You were lucky to get a nod as a hello from him. Other than that, there isn't anything I've ever seen or heard that would lead me to believe that he isn't straight. He is definitely straight, in my opinion. Other than his overly inflated ego, he's pretty cool, and most everyone seems to admire him.

KURT RUSSELL
Packin' (LG)

I saw a lot of Kurt at Lions Spa the year the story broke in the tabloids when they caught him coming out of the spa and claimed he was cheating on Goldie Hawn with masseuses. From what I heard, and from my own recollections, that was all true. In my opinion, Kurt Russell is definitely straight. I never saw him do anything Goldie would be upset about, but I heard things she definitely would not like to hear.

Apparently, Kurt had been getting massages from Sarah in room six, with full release included. Full release to most is commonly referred to as the "happy ending." Kurt was seemingly addicted to her, because they said he was seeing her almost every day. This was right about the time the story broke about him at the spa. I've seen with my own two eyes and experienced Sarah in room six with her optional full release massage. Let me tell you, she knows what she's doing. I could definitely see where a straight guy could get hooked on her persuasive ways, but for me, a basically gay guy, I remember when she thought I was straight and offered me the full release after a massage. I was horny, and my dick was hard, so I said yes. If she hadn't grabbed it right then and there, I may have had to. Besides, what's thirty dollars, right? Point is, I knew what Kurt was getting first-hand, so I know what he was going through, and it was pure pleasure at the hands of Sarah. Literally.

Whenever I'd see Kurt at the spa, he was either coming or going. There was only one time that I saw him naked. He was in the shower, and I have been a fan ever since. Wow! Kurt Russell is packin'. Now I can see what Goldie sees in the Disney star.

Kurt had quite the reputation at the spa for liking the ladies and their massaging skills. Some of the gay guys would go crazy when they would see Kurt. They would talk in the steam room about how much they wanted to suck his big dick. Unfortunately, the gays knew Kurt didn't go that way, and they hated it. No man-on-man for Kurt. He is only into the ladies, and from what I've heard, he hasn't been back to the spa since the story came out on him years ago.

So it looks like the only lady he's into these days is Goldie Hawn (or at least he has learned you never know who's watching) and he's being much more careful now. I hope it's the former of the two. I hope he is being true to Goldie. Now, I have also heard Goldie was not upset about Kurt and the massage girl, but instead was upset that it played out in the tabloids. The rumor mills have it that the couple has an open relationship and it has always been that way. Moreover, they are very happy with it. Like I always say…whatever makes you happy!

PAULY SHORE
Lackin' (SM)

Pauly Shore was one of the first celebrities I met at City Spa. He's an interesting character. Many people say he's gay, but I don't think so. Sure, I caught him looking at the spa-goers all the time, but I never witnessed any behavior that would make me think he's gay. Maybe he's gay curious. With Pauly, it was always hot or cold, never in between. Sometimes, he would be so nice and talkative, and at other times, he would stare you down as if you had stolen something.

The way we met was, he was coming off his MTV success and just starting his movie career. The staff, and members frequenting the spa, would always make fun of him. He was like the joke of the spa who was starting to find some success in his life, yet still, most definitely, was on the D-list compared to all the A-listers who went to City Spa. When he'd be steaming, he would always be talking that "dude" talk. As I said, I don't think he's gay, but everyone always cracked jokes about him as though he was. To hear him speak, I have to admit, he does sound gay.

As his career was progressing, people at the club seemed to treat him with a little more respect. But, much like his short-lived career, whenever a true celebrity was around, Pauly would always do major ass-kissing. He was always going on and on about his upcoming projects. He just seemed odd to me.

Regardless of his career choices, he definitely chose City Spa to visit almost daily. It wasn't a rarity to see him a couple of times a week parading around with a towel on his head. He stopped being personable and friendly around the time he was starring in *Son in Law*. He was so full of himself. The more popular he became, the stranger the looks he would give a person. For years we wouldn't even acknowledge each other's presence. Now, he's most definitely back on Earth, where he's always belonged, especially since his fifteen minutes of fame have passed.

Presently, Pauly manages his mother's comedy club on Sunset. I went to see a Jaguar for sale once. When I got there, it turned out that it was Pauly's mother's car, Mitzi Shore, whom I've always liked. I was viewing his mother's $4,000 car, and, for some reason, I could sense he was embarrassed. I ended up not buying the car that day, and we've never spoken since. I'm sure the feelings are mutual, no love lost there. Nevertheless, I wish him well.

The only thing I might add about Pauly that was odd, even strange, was one week you'd see him at the spa naked and thin, and then, a few weeks later, you would see him really fat and swollen with C-cup man boobs. I think he's a binge eater. His weight has seemingly fluctuated from severe weight gain to normal weight gain in recent photos. He looks like he's eating a lot again.

JEAN-CLAUDE VAN DAMME
Packin' (MD)

In L.A., the guys all have the same look and behavior when they are on drugs. They are gaunt and sexually off the meter, cruising for sex at the spas, and Van Damme was no exception to the rule. Long before I met the great action star Jean-Claude Van Damme, I had heard many dirty stories about his bad-boy behavior and his reputation. It certainly did precede him. In person, he is a far cry from the big hero on the screen that he so often portrayed back in his heyday. In fact, he is very small in stature. By the time I met him, he was long past his glory days in Hollywood and looked rather sickly in person. At first, I thought he might have AIDS, but the more I was around him, the more I could tell his overly thin, sickly look was self-induced from drugs. In fact, he more than lived up to all the stories I had heard about him. He still has a nice body, much leaner now, and his dick is nice.

The first time I met him, he offered to suck me off. I probably would have let him, but he looked sick, so I declined. However, I did stay in the steam room with him and masturbated. Before long, there were a bunch of guys in there with us. At one point, Jean-Claude was fucking this little Asian guy in front of us all. Van Damme is very verbal while in the throes of passion. He kept telling the Asian guy to open his fuckhole more and to take all his cock in his ass. Guys were blowing their loads all over the place, myself included. He was a complete freak. Van Damme told another guy to fuck him while he fucked the Asian. The other guy gladly complied. Jean-Claude didn't even blink when the guy shoved his huge cock up his ass. This was certainly not his first time at this kind of rodeo.

One of the regular gays for hire who frequented Century Spa blabbed to anyone who would listen about his hookups with Van Damme. He claimed that whenever he would get a call from Jean-Claude to get together, it was always the same routine. He said he would get six eight balls of cocaine, pick up a lot of porno, booze, and cigarettes, and bring along a well-hung friend and a smoking-hot female. They would all hang out at Van Damme's house in Studio City when his wife and kids would be gone for little getaways. He would party at home, in the Valley, with basically complete strangers and have unprotected sex orgies for days at a time. No wonder he always looked so sickly when I would see him at the spa. He was a die-hard partier, and it showed. He has absolutely no inhibitions about sex and performing in front of people.

There was a period of time when Van Damme was at the spa all the time. And every time it was the same thing. He was in one of the saunas getting fucked or doing the fucking. Word would spread throughout the spa so fast that before you knew it, there wouldn't even be standing room. I would just watch and wonder how these stars could be so out of control in a public place. It just never made any sense to me. Why not just go to a hotel and order up some sex to your room and play it safe? I guess that is the real zillion-dollar question. And, as always, before long, Edward, the owner's son, would be snooping his perverted nose in to watch as well.

You would think that being the owner's son, you would break up the sex show going on in your sauna. But not Edward. He loved it, and promoted it on the Internet, so that guys would know if they wanted to fuck or be fucked by a celebrity, his spa was the place to be. And, just as he planned, the place was packed, and Edward was laughing all the way to the bank.

The last time I witnessed Jean-Claude having sex, it got a little crazy in the steam room. Before I knew it, this guy came running out screaming that there were faggots in there getting fucked and he was repulsed. Right then, Van Damme ran out of the steam room, headed to his locker to get dressed and get the hell out of there. He did it so fast, it would have made your head spin. Personally, I was thrilled this straight guy had the balls to do that. He was like, *"Enough already!"*

I never saw Van Damme there again after that. Maybe he got the message that it was a health spa, not a bathhouse. There is a huge difference.

Steve, the gay for hire, said he was still putting parties together for Van Damme whenever his family was out of town. Except, these days, he was ordering a lot of Viagra for Van Damme. Apparently, all that coke had taken a toll on his dick, and he couldn't get it up, but once he discovered Viagra, he was off to the races again.

BILLY ZANE
Packin' (XLG)

I met him before the movie *Titanic* came out, back around 1995, shortly after I became a member at City Spa. He was very approachable back then, and although I had been told he was gay from other spa members, I personally didn't see anything back then to lead me to believe what I heard was true.

Years later, I would run into him a lot at Century Spa, where I would see many things that contradicted what I had previously thought. He seemed to enjoy running around naked with that huge cock of his. One of my friends from the spa, who is gay, told me that he and Zane had hooked up several times. His details included that Zane is definitely a top and that they had even had a threesome with another person at Zane's house. There were several times where I walked in on Billy Zane while he and others were jacking off in the steam room. All the guys were after Billy and his humongous dick. It appeared to me he enjoyed being watched while getting down and dirty.

When naked, Billy Zane looks like a Greek god. No wonder all the boys wanted to be with him. He would go from one steam room to another, and if you sat back and watched, you could see a small group of boys following him throughout the spa. Sometimes, on occasion, there would be a larger following, like naked paparazzi. Only they weren't after the big story; it was Zane's donkey dick they were chasing. It was, without doubt, a sight to see.

Sometimes they'd get their big story, too! When there was a nice group of sexy guys after him, and once Zane was done with his steam, the naked paparazzi would follow him into the back room, where they would all have sex together. Sex, my ass, it was a full-blown orgy! After Zane was done with the boys, he would take a quick shower and be gone faster than he had come in.

How do I know what was going on in that back room? The orgy participants would come back to the steam rooms and tell us all about what they had done with Billy Zane. The hot topic was always how big his dick was and how he was such a stud. They couldn't stop talking about how he could go on and on. I remember one time, one of the guys said when Billy shot his load, it flew across the room. Everyone laughed. Exaggeration? Maybe, maybe not. I know one thing. Every time he entered the spa, guys would gather together and follow him. He must have been doing something right!

Whenever I would see Billy, it was pretty much always the same thing. He'd be running around showing off his dick and disappearing into dark rooms with men. There were a lot of gays who would go to Century Spa looking for him specifically for that purpose. Even the new gays to the spa would ask me if I ever saw Billy Zane there, and if I knew when he was normally around.

It was rumored that whenever Zane or Travolta was there, the owner's son, Edward, would put it online to drum up additional business for his spa. It worked, too. The word would spread online, and the next thing you knew, guys were coming in saying they just saw it online that Zane or Travolta was going to be there. As the years passed, it appeared that Billy Zane had become an Englishman. Whenever he would speak, he sounded as though he was from England. Very proper in his speech…but not so proper with his sexcapades.

JOHN TRAVOLTA
PACKIN' (LG)

It wouldn't be right for me to rate all the other celebrities penises without rating my all-time favorite. John Travolta. With its bulging flesh and pulsing veins, this is the true definition of the Italian stallion. Forget rocky! The moment you see Travolta's cock, your jaw will drop. If he hadn't gone in the direction he did, he could have definitely done porn, and had quite a following. Does John Holmes ring a bell? They say a man loses an inch of penile length with every ten pounds he gains. That, certainly, does not apply to J.T.

THE END

EPILOGUE

I had a lot of fun hanging out with stars and observing their unique personalities and behaviors for years. During those years at the spas I began to notice that the gays were foregoing looking for steams and sex in the gay bath houses and began cruising for straight men at straight spas. They were methodical with a common purpose, had their own style, and even their own vernacular. This had become a "gay spa subculture" to say the least. Add movie and TV stars to the mix and you just know all hell is going to break lose. This subculture has taken over so many straight spas, it's nearly an epidemic and it is not going anywhere anytime soon.

A couple of years have passed since I have step foot in a public or private spa for a relaxing steam. As an alternative, I had a spa installed in the safety of my own home. It's not as exciting as sitting with lots of Hollywood big wigs pulling on their big dicks, but at least the days of getting hit on for sex while trying to enjoy a steam were long gone. Not only that, but I knew once the word got out about my book, a public spa was the last place I wanted to be unless I wanted another near-death beating. I was still attempting to recover from the last savage beating I so luckily survived. I'll never forget the day when I was trying to re-familiarize myself with using a computer when my dear friend, Lorrie Llamas, walked into the room.

"Robert, you are trying to learn how to use a computer again, maybe you should write a story. Your story!", she said.

"What do you mean, my story?", I asked.

"The one you've shared with me. You know, about how you had dreams of being John Travolta's boyfriend and all the things you saw and heard over the 15 years you were there as a member. You could include the beating and how the owner turned his back on you after you were assaulted in his spa. Lucky for him you didn't sue the bastard!", she continued.

She seemed more enthusiastic over the idea of me writing a book than I was. I had never thought about writing a book. Especially one about revealing the true realities of so many loved and adored celebrities. Could I write about all I had seen at the spa? What if someone got ahold of this book, then what?, I began to ask myself. What are people going to think of me for writing the book? All of these things came to mind and I pondered over them for months. On the seventh month, I decided to put Lorrie's words into action. I went out, bought a laptop and began what has now become "You'll Never Spa In This Town Again". Little by little my computer skills returned and slowly but surely I was on my way.

I never set out to OUT John Travolta or anyone else mentioned in my book, but I certainly was not going to rearrange the truth just because there were celebrities involved. While contemplating whether or not to write a book, one of my main standpoints was to write my story based on absolute truths and that is what I did. These celebrities were living a lie. They were out in the open doing things that I'm sure their fans and followers would want to know about so I included their shenanigans in my book. Besides, anyone with reasonable intelligence knows the best way to keep one's life private is to stay out of the limelight. Instead, these celebs paraded their sexual exploits in front of strangers, apparently, without any concern that it might come back to haunt them.

Unlike those who made up lies about Travolta, my story is true. All the dates are here, and all the facts shine through

ACKNOWLEDGEMENTS

Due to the content of my book, very few people were involved in putting it all together. Some were intimidated and thought they'd be killed by Travolta and/or his Scientology clan leaving me with a real conundrum of where to turn for assistance. Whereas most authors could thank their agent, editor, art director, and co-author, I didn't have any of those. However, I was blessed to have all my needs met with bringing *"You'll Never Spa In This Town Again"* to life.

I particularly want to express my sincere gratitude to the dearest friend I've ever had, Lorrie V. Llamas who encouraged me to write my story.

I'd also like to include Charles Karpinski for a lifetime of loyalty, friendship, and support throughout the process of getting my story told and for being such a wonderful friend to my mother, Patty.

To my dear friend and dentist Aristotle Corkos, you have become the brother I always longed for. Your friendship and loyalty has been a blessing to my life. Thank you for keeping me smiling.

My Dali and Dazi, what more can I say about my two girls. I love them with all my heart. It is a pleasure and a gift to be spending my life with them.

To my parents, Robert and Patricia Davis, who not only gave me life but gave me the strength to overcome obstacles and always see the good in everyone. I would especially like to thank my mother "Patty" who was along for this Travolta ride right from the beginning, and paid for countless massages and spa memberships to make this journey possible.

Thanks to Peter for lending an ear when I most definitely needed someone to be there just to listen.

To Francine Smiderly, I want to thank you for all your support from day one, including the countless emails of information as the result of your endless hours of research.

To Boris and Ilya Gorovatsky, I thank you for your constant encouragement and input in my life and dreams.

Thanks to my attorney, G. Scott Sobel, who has had my back since our professional relationship began and who is not only a great guy but has turned mad dogs into whimpering puppies all while protecting my freedom of speech and thereby reminding me that I have every right to tell my story..

To Fernanda Hinkle, thank you so much for letting me run so many things by you and always getting right back to me with your wisdom and research.

To Golden and Timbol Lawfirm. I knew I was in extremely confident hands from our first meeting. Your firm is so warm and caring to all who pass through your doors. I feel fortunate to have made your acquaintance.

With extreme gratitude, I want to thank Ocy Hinkle for being a friend and for sticking by me throughout this entire process. Even death threats, being followed by blacked out vehicles didn't deter him from standing by me and getting this book done. He was on call, around the clock, utilizing his computer skills and technical know-how and everything in between, even providing additional security. Nothing seemed to deter him from helping me and I'm sincerely grateful. Without his invaluable help, *"You'll Never Spa In This Town Again"* may have never made it to the light of day.

Last, but not least, I want to thank all of the thousands of Travolta fans who took the time to email me expressing their excitement about my upcoming book. I was touched beyond belief to hear from so many complete strangers telling me how proud they were of me for having the strength to tell my story. To all of you, I say thank you from the bottom of my heart. Your words of encouragement carried me through.

"TRACKING TRAVOLTA"
COMING SOON

News of my book spread like wildfire and, before I knew it, I was inundated with emails from countless men all over the world who had stories they wanted to share with me about their sexual romps with John Travolta and Kelly, too. Yes...Kelly. They weren't just giving me dates, times, and information. They were requesting for me to include their stories in "You'll Never Spa In This Town Again". I was shocked to read emails from reliable sources about Kelly's sexcapades and the many adventures she has accompanied her husband on. Even repeatedly sharing the same employee! This peek into the Travolta's personal life away from the spas provided by a Travolta family insider who shares more stories with me that you just have to read for yourself. She wasn't the only one either. Several people saying the same things about her and her complete support of his sexual adventures along with details that do not leave much for the imagination.

After receiving so many emails I decided to make a collection of them all and put them in the form of a book called "Tracking Travolta". This book will showcase the most interesting and shocking stories along with an interview between myself and the sources. You will certainly come away feeling like you know the real Travoltas versus the projected Hollywood image they would like you all to believe they are.

THE TRUTH BEHIND THE 2009 ROYAL CARIBBEAN ENCHANTMENT OF THE SEAS CRUISE

John Travolta separated from his wife, Kelly Preston, in June 2009 and headed for fun in the sun on a five-day Caribbean cruise aboard the Royal Carribean's Enchantment of the Seas cruise. Travolta and his handlers would like you to believe that Mr. Travolta jumped ship early to return home to try and reconcile with his beloved wife. The truth of the matter is, John Travolta was ordered to leave the ship after sexually propositioning and nearly sexually assaulting one of the ships employees while the "Swordfish" star was naked as a jaybird. Travolta offered the employee thousands of dollars to have sex with him. Stunned and in complete horror, the employee fled from Travolta's stateroom number 8520, and ran to his superiors to report the lewd sexual attack he had just escaped from. So while JT was telling the world, he couldn't go on after the death of his son, Jett, it would appear that things were in full swing . Pun intended.

The Royal Caribbean employee that was accosted by John Travolta is here in the states and he is going to share his shocking and truthful story in graphic detail. A first person account from the victim himself exposing the real Travolta for who he really is. You can read his unbelievable and disturbing account of the aggressive sexual assault making him one of many who felt trapped and helpless against Travolta's advances. As a result of him refusing Travolta's advances and lucrative offer of money for sex, his career with Royal Caribbean was ruined and his life was turned upside down. Another life ruined at the hands of Travolta!

This is just one of hundreds of emails from people that truly know the Travoltas When you're done reading my upcoming book, *"Tracking Travolta"*, you too will feel like you finally, after all this time, know them for who they really are.

CPSIA information can be obtained at www.ICGtesting.com
Printed in the USA
LVOW05s1540161213

365565LV00032B/1581/P